Toward Saving
The Honeybee

Günther Hauk

BIODYNAMIC FARMING AND GARDENING ASSOCIATION

2002

Printed in the United States of America by Thomson-Shore, Inc.

ISBN: 0-938250-1490000

First Edition

Permission to print the following illustrations has been graciously granted by:
Dadant & Sons, Inc.: pages 28, 34, and 40, and corresponding color plates;
Guenther Mancke: page 14, "Hanging Chains";
Karen Emerson: pages 21 and 31 and corresponding color plates;
The author: p. 15, 17, 18, 42, 46, 50, 58, 64, 66 and corresponding color plates.

Acknowledgements

For the depth of insights into the honeybee's nature I am most profoundly indebted to Rudolf Steiner's grand *oeuvre* with which he has inspired countless individuals in every facet of human endeavor.

This book would certainly not be as readable were it not for the editing efforts carried out with expertise and love by Judith Rissenberg.

My deep gratitude also goes out to the Biodynamic Farming and Gardening Associationon on the one hand for generously supporting my work and research at The Pfeiffer Center as well as for publishing the book, and on the other hand to Bruce Bumbarger for his professional advice and patience in getting the book into a pleasing shape and form.

Contents

Introduction 9

1 The Hive: Form & Substance 13

2 Wax 20

3 Queen, Workers, Drones 25

4 Swarming 37

5 Honey and Pollen 44

6 Health, Parasites, Diseases, & Treatments 48

7 Outlook 61

APPENDIX A: Formic, Oxalic, & Lactic Acid Treatments 67

APPENDIX B: Foulbrood 73

REFERENCES 75

Introduction

In times of crisis our consciousness soars to new heights, enabling us to rise up to challenges, to take action previously not possible. An impending threat to our well-being wakes us up from a comfortable sleep into the reality of potential danger.

Crises, then, can be good, and are potentially some of our best teachers! They are always filled with latent possibilities for change, for healing, for evolving.

One could say that the majority of our global population is generally asleep to the significant danger that currently exists within our Earth's ecosystem. There is a crisis of environmental distress that shows itself from the depletion of the soil to the pollution of our waters and atmosphere, to the prevailing abuse of plant and animal kingdoms. A widespread increase of illness, weakened immunity and increasing occurrences of natural disasters reflects the imbalance that threatens to destroy many forms of life as we know them, including the health and stability of our own lives.

The insatiable demands of a materialist technology have somehow crucially diminished our reverence and compassion for various forms of life and thwarted our understanding of the web of interdependence that weaves our own life together with the other kingdoms. In the haste of our modernized pursuits, we have put aside the question: what is necessary for the welfare of the 'other' being, what is health imbibing and what might be detrimental to its nature?

To rediscover this relinquished path of reverence and the fruits that develop out of a deeper understanding of this other being is a task that lies before us when we deal with all of life. In his novel *Truth and Fiction*, the poet and scientist Johann Wolfgang von Goethe expressed this ideal as a pedagogical province where the student learns: to develop reverence for those beings above us, those at the same level, and those below us (Goethe 1902). One could articulate this code of ethics even further: to experience reverence for those above us; to cultivate true friendship toward our fellow human beings; and to protect and nurture those below us: the animals, the plants, the entire earth.

It is becoming increasingly clear to a growing number of individuals that what we call health is really a reflection of 'life force', not the absence of one or the other bacterium, virus or fungus. And that this state of being called health is dependent upon many subtle but powerful interconnections among all the internal workings of an organism, and their relationship with the microcosmic and macrocosmic environmental influences.

If we begin to examine our level of consciousness regarding the health of the animal world, we are in for some rather shocking revelations. For example, the life expectancy of a cow has dropped from twenty to twenty–five years down to five or six years; the state of health of the rest of our domestic animals is abominable, to say the least. Their immune systems have been weakened to such a degree that without large doses of antibacterial treatments most of them are unable to survive. We have forgotten that the word animal comes from the Greek word *anima*, meaning 'soul' as well as 'movement'.

An animal has emotions, feelings and needs movement in order to be healthy (even the sloth!). When we coop up these animals, lock them up, and prevent them from living in accordance with their true nature, this causes them immense suffering, a suffering of which they cannot speak verbally, but which is communicated through their eyes, their behavior, their state of health.

The bee is no exception. It, too, is a sick patient who has been trying for years to signal to us the deep crises of its diminishing life forces and its increasing inability to resonate with the environment. Statistics speak very loudly, especially those gathered over the past forty years. In the recent decades of the 1960s and 1970s, waves of massive death rates of bee colonies were reported in Europe. This puzzled the professional and hobbyist beekeepers quite deeply. During the next decade, the varroa mite, imported from the Far East, claimed an increasing number of hives, and beekeepers lost between half to two–thirds and in some cases *all of their colonies* in a single year! The same pattern repeated itself in America a few years later. In 1996 the newspapers reported that approximately sixty percent of the honeybees in the United States had been lost; some states showed losses up to ninety percent. Expressed in numbers, that means a decrease of colonies from seven million to two-and-a-half million! With an average colony numbering 50,000 worker bees in the summer, this loss has quite an impact on many facets of nature in addition to the activity of pollination.

Major questions are raised: can we find the reasons for this devastation that happened to the inherently healthy, productive honeybee? And what can be done to correct, or at least to begin to remedy, this crisis?

It is noteworthy that in 1923 the Austrian scientist, poet, philosopher and spiritual scientist Rudolf Steiner (1861-1925) presented a series of lectures about bees in which he gave, out of his spiritual research, tremendous insights into the nature of this wonderful creature (Steiner 1998). At that time certain forms of modern beekeeping (including the queen breeding method which we have 'perfected' today) had been in effect for a few decades. Dr. Steiner mentioned, even at that time, that the honeybee might not survive the end of the twentieth century if these methods were continued. A beekeeper attending his lectures vehemently opposed this prediction. Steiner's response suggested that such things could not be noticed right away. "Let's talk to each other again in one hundred years, Mr. Mueller; then we'll see what kind of opinion you'll have at that point. This is something that can't be decided today" (Steiner 1998, 74).

He could make such a prediction because he could look beneath the surface, beyond the viewpoints and techniques involved with quick results. We have arrived at a time where we come close to verifying his statement.

Of course, when the varroa mite entered the scene of the bee crisis, it seemed most natural to put all the blame on it as the main cause of devastation. It was as if the varroa mite became the acclaimed villain, the enemy of the bee population and all that was necessary was to eliminate this dangerous pest! Technology found yet another entry into the bees' domain: antibiotics and antidotes were quickly manufactured to eliminate the mites. This, however, has not resolved the dilemma. Strangely enough, bees are still dying today despite these newly developed suppressants. Other strategies are being tried as well. Various oils, such as peppermint and fennel, have been used with some success. Some people are hoping to breed a bee that can cope with the varroa mite just as the honeybee in the Far East has been doing for centuries, if not millennia.

Other health problems continue to plague the bee population; not only varroa mites, but also tracheal mites, foulbrood, intestinal illness and, as of late, the hive beetle – all of these have been working on decimating the bee colonies. Is it possible to eliminate all of these illnesses and impediments to the bees' health with a cure-all solution? Or is the honeybee, in fact, trying to tell us something? It is, in fact, screaming to us through its overwhelming illness and fatality statistics, **that it is not merely a mite or some other 'invader', but in fact our whole approach to its existence** that has continued to weaken it and caused its health and resistance to deteriorate.

With this in mind, **we come to the aim of this book, which is to raise our awareness regarding all facets of beekeeping in relation to the honeybee's health:** forms, substances and materials for hives; the breeding of queens and the treatment of queens, workers and drones; the significance of swarming, the importance of virgin wax production, and the need for hygienic and holistic approaches toward parasites and diseases.

This book is *not* a substitute for a good, solid introduction to beekeeping. However, it is hoped that the presentation of this material and the perspectives regarding our responsibility as caretakers and stewards of these amazing creatures will encourage a deeper understanding of the bee as a very sensitive and powerful environmental barometer, and thereby instill in us a higher consciousness and conscientiousness in relation to beekeeping practices. It is also hoped that as our awareness increases, we as individuals will find the courage to 'swim against the stream', and to promote among each other nurturing, healthful, harmonious methods for raising bees; methods that will, in turn, reflect a true reverence for the interrelationship and interdependency that we share with all living beings on the Earth.

Then we will truly be able to turn our exploitation and destruction of nature into life sustaining and life ennobling practices.

1

The Hive:
Form and Substance

In a temperate climate the honeybee needs housing for warmth and protection, for unlike the wasp, it cannot build that outer sheath by itself. When bees live in the wild, they are free to find residence in the crevice of a rock wall or inside a hollow tree. However, as the honeybee became domesticated, men found and developed other types of homes for them. As early as pre-historic times, mankind possessed an instinct for habitat, and showed an intuitive sense for the effects of forms on living beings. By perceiving the nature of the bee it was obvious to these peoples that a round shape was appropriate for a hive. Through study and observation, we can now conclude that early man was quite perceptive and correctly understood the instinctual nature of bees and their innate 'architectural' requirements for a healthy and productive beehive.

One way to understand the importance of a round form for the bee is to realize that almost all of its significant life experiences and expression manifest in 'roundness', for example:
- the queen cell is sack-like;
- the six-sided cells of the workers and drones are the most economical way of placing a lot of round cells close to each other in a given space so that no empty spaces remain;
- the queen lays eggs in circles, moving from comb to comb;
- the comb itself takes on a beautiful heart shape which is the result of a round structure under the influence of gravity (the law of hanging chains gives this form; see following page);
- the winter cluster, the flight of the swarm, and the rotation of the larvae spinning its cocoon all take place in roundness or at least an approximation of roundness.

13

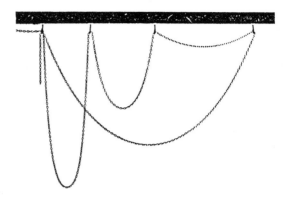

Illustration of the law of hanging chains (Mancke & Csarnietzki 1996)

In esoteric knowledge, roundness is an expression of the life forces. Roundness represents warmth, health, productivity, radiance and an overall energetic resonance with life. It promotes harmony and facilitates fertility and abundance in both the nature of its shape, and by the energetic emanation of the shape. The cube or rectangle, on the other hand, is connected esoterically to the mineral element, relating to the hardening forces of the mineral world. Here we find sharpness, angularity, a sense of cutting and splitting through space, which is indicated in the nature of the forms themselves.

When did the concept of a rectangular hive emerge into the beekeeping world? It is recorded that while the Romans experimented with rectangular forms for bees, the Egyptians and Germanic peoples continued to use round structures. In some countries like Tunisia and the Dominican Republic, just to name two examples, the round hive continues to be used. In Europe, round skeps were housing bee colonies until the middle of the twentieth century. Nevertheless, the rectangular box is, admittedly, very convenient and practical. Its use spread in Europe in the eighteenth and especially in the nineteenth century after a German priest, T. Christ, recommended its practicality and ease of handling. Since it was simpler to build and use, and since nobody seemed to have asked the bee whether she felt supported by its angularity, the use of the rectangular hive was not questioned at all.

Although our own dwellings are almost always rectangular,

we can experience the difference that various forms have on us. Have you ever attended a performance in a round theater, or spent a night in a round room? Certainly the latter is challeng-ing when placing furniture! Have you ever been in a round kindergarten room radiating protective warmth simply by its form? Have you ever seen a rectangular nest?

The question of form really has to do with the purpose of a structure; there is nothing negative to say about the rectangle in general. But one could agree that a round home for a bee colony would provide a tangible quality of nest warmth and be supportive of the 'roundabout' way in which the bees live their lives. With a round structure, there are no cold, damp corners in winter and spring to deal with! However, one thing is clear: this approach is *not* as comfortable and practical for us beekeepers! Therein lies the dilemma. And since the honeybee is such an adaptable creature, making the best of just about any situation, why should we worry about the form of the hive at all? Or could it very well be, that at this point a factor such as the form of a hive *has* to be taken into consideration for raising the health and vitality of our ailing friends?

Another very important factor, complementary to the form of the hive, is the substance or quality of material from which the hive is made. Bees, because they are involved in a constant interactive and reciprocal relationship to the substances creating their abode, require something that supports their life forces in

Freshly built heart-shaped comb with honey

15

order to perform their task in harmony and health. It is easy for us, in our contemporary lifestyle, to overlook the unique, interactive relationship that various substances provide to the greater and smaller environment. In our daily lives we seldom think about the role of substances chemically interacting in the air; or, in a sense, the 'nutritional', the nurturing and nourishing essence of air and light and their effects upon living beings. We do become aware, however, of these interrelationships, when the effects are so strong that it can be scientifically verified that our health is impaired (e.g., when exposed to formaldehyde in building materials, lead in paints). Extremely minute quantities are sufficient to cause damage.

The typical wooden hive boxes currently in use are usually painted white for the protection of the wood and to reflect the sunlight, providing a cooler dwelling. The long-term effects of the paints and glues on the health of the bees have not been researched since it is very difficult to come to conclusive evidence unless the effect of the poison is very obvious and observable in the short-term. However, we are accumulating an increasing amount of evidence that reveals how the effectiveness of substances can be very great, even in extremely small, homeopathic quantities. Thus Ehrenfried Pfeiffer quotes research results where the effectiveness of substances even in minute dilutions of 1:1,000, 000 has been proven (Pfeiffer 1983, 1:11–12; Kolisko 1978).

Just as certain substances cause illness, even death, by their mere presence, there are others that are exceptionally valuable in strengthening the life force and the vitality of living beings. The ideal substances for a beehive would have to give insulation and, at the same time, provide a 'breathable' quality, not shutting out the subtle energies and influences of all that streams in from the smaller and greater environment. Wood certainly is good on both counts. Although the ancient Romans used wood for their hives, the Roman historian Columella also reports that the best hives were made of reed or cork. Did the beekeepers at that time perceive things that we are no longer aware of?

Straw was and, in some countries, still is used for building hives. Rudolf Steiner mentions that straw, "by its nature, attracts from the air very different substances than wood does" (Steiner 1998, 85). Of all the various straws, rye straw, according to Matthias Thun, has the ability to attract the greatest amount of silica, thus increasing the stability and warming quality to the bees' home (Thun 1986, 57). Another substance that has been used in building houses for people as well as skeps for bees (and is just being rediscovered!) comes from an animal that has amazing metabolic life forces, has fertilized and enlivened the soil for millennia, and is still considered holy in certain cultures: the cow. The beautifully digested grasses, clovers, and healing herbs that are the ingredients of the cow dung have excellent insulating properties and after drying, the dung loses its smell completely. Do the dogs that just love to roll and 'bathe' in this substance know something about the healing and vitalizing qualities of the cow dung? It is noteworthy that throughout history, from early times to the Romans to the present, some of the most readily accepted, nurturing hive bodies have been made out of clay, cow dung and straw. Such a hive provides a comfortable, harmonious home that sustains the bees through summer and winter months equally well.

I am fully aware of the fact that a round hive made of these substances will not attract the fancy of many people at this time. One has to overcome one's fear of being considered crazy or eccentric. At this point every small aspect contributing to the overall health and vitality of our sick patient, the honeybee, can be appreciated and put into practice. **This is not a call for everyone to build round hives out of these substances.** This special nurturing effort is difficult to expect from the professional beekeeper with hundreds, if not

Round straw/clay/cow-dung hives

Horizontal hexagonal hive built by Tom Wilkinson

thousands of colonies. But perhaps the hobbyist beekeeper, after gaining experience with the rectangular hive box (which is definitely easier to work with) could make this extra effort and provide one or two 'special care' stations for our great friends and benefactors. There is definitely a great reward in seeing the beauty of these rounded, heart-shaped combs with gentle undulations, and in perceiving a rise in the vitality of the colonies.

If we allow ourselves the opportunity to enter into the world of the bees and to consider as well the various qualities that are inherent to certain forms, we may discover yet another way to incorporate the beneficial harmony or roundness with the practicality of what is rectangular. We may find, through continued experimentation, that the structural forces of a pentagonal or hexagonal shape may also be useful. Beekeepers in different areas of the world are working at designing 'THE Hive', a hive that can accommodate the innate instincts and naturally occurring activities of the bees so that they may live in a health-imbibing surrounding; one that retains a degree of practicality for the beekeeper; and one that answers as well to the needs of our times, the needs of healing and true stewardship.

At this time, in association with The Pfeiffer Center, research is under way with several types of experimental hives: round hives made of clay, rye straw and cow dung; pentagonal and hexagonal – vertical as well as horizontal – hives made of wood. These short-term, newly begun experimentations have not been operating long enough to provide convincing 'statistical' proof; yet what has been experienced so far in the continued search for a nurturing hive-shape gives rise to hope.

In summary, we could formulate questions relating to the hive form and substance in the following way: Let us regain more sensitivity for the intangible but existing effects that forms, as catalysts for energy fields, have on all living beings. Substances are never just substances alone but always carriers of forces. Their predominantly subtle effects, whether positive or negative, are not easily verified, especially in our sped up culture. Nevertheless, we should increasingly take these into consideration. Therefore I would never put my bees into a hive made of synthetic materials, nor myself into synthetic underwear.

We don't want to return to old ways of beekeeping but rather penetrate with new insights whatever we venture to do.

2

Wax

Beeswax, the product of an animal that has been considered sacred in almost every culture throughout history, is indeed a very special and precious substance. It has been used with great reverence in many religions for ceremony and ritual. The aesthetic beauty, the fragrance, and the multitude of uses that beeswax offers to man are in themselves accomplishments. The bee, in its simplest acts of life, reveals to us a constant stream of wondrous synthesis, industriousness and transformation.

Whereas other types of bees and wasps use materials from nature to build their combs (living plants, earth, old wood), the honeybee alone creates the substance for the comb in her own body, out of her bloodstream. We can marvel at the significance of the bees' nourishment, which is the nectar of flowers – the finest of substances produced by the plant. This sap or nectar results from a unique combination – a synthesis – of physical substances (mostly oxygen, hydrogen, carbon, nitrogen) together with that cosmic force that enables all life on this planet: *light.*

It is this purest and most ennobled of food substances that the bee ingests, assimilates and converts into bee 'substances', including blood. Just as our bones crystallize out of our bloodstream – (beautiful to observe in the growing embryo) – so the bee's blood is transformed into wax that is 'sweated' out in thin, wafer-like, almost translucent white plates on the underside of her abdomen. It is estimated that it takes approximately five pounds of honey to produce one pound of wax! This pure white wax is used to make those marvelously light but extremely stable combs – combs which on the one hand provide a place where new life grows, is nourished, and matures into the finished insect; and on the other hand, provide the storage places for honey and pollen. The honeycomb, when inhabited and warmed by the bees, is pliable and has a certain radiance, a liveliness to it. Without the warmth of the bees to keep it soft, it loses its luster and becomes brittle and dull.

One can compare this amazing rhythmic process of wax 'production' to the forming of our bones, which 'flake out' of our bloodstream and then become hard enough to support us, yet remain alive and flexible. Consider the constant change that our bones undergo in their inner complex structure depending upon the amount of pressure and weight they receive as a result of our exertion or inactivity. A second parallel can be drawn to the fact that bones are the place of constant renewal of life, of the red blood cells.

To consider that these combs are a kind of outer skeleton which the bees create to live on and live in, is an idea that has powerful reality when considering the processes involved, for without the honeycomb, the colony is doomed to perish in a relatively short time.

Following this train of thought, we can begin to appreciate that *the production of wax is of major significance* to the bees, for it rep–resents a constant renewal; it guarantees health and stability. The wax cells, wherein the queen places her eggs, are what the womb is for our offspring – a sacred place. Just as we derive our strength to a great degree from the health and stability of our bones (for walking, jumping, running, lifting, etc.), so does the bee derive her strength to raise healthy offspring from the substance that the bee has 'sacrificed' from her own body, this precious wax.

Comb built without foundation

How do *we* presently value this vital substance? We have, in the name of productivity, decided to 'save' the bee from putting all this effort into wax production; after all, it's the honey we are after – as much as we can possibly harvest! So the wax foundation has been invented as an efficiency measure for beekeepers. This thin sheet of wax from melted combs has the exact structure of the base of the six-sided cells imprinted on it and is wired into a frame to give it stability. The bees use part of this wax for drawing out the cells and then proceed to finish the comb by supplementing the remainder that is required out of their own newly created wax.

There are basically two serious problems with this modernized way of reducing wax production. One is that wax as a substance naturally retains all the accumulated chemicals as well as the spores of certain diseases. The latter are killed by heating the wax to approximately 260 degrees Fahrenheit; the former are still present in the foundations. With our conventional agriculture, most of these chemicals are poisons that are aimed at killing life. The suffix '-cide' means death: homicide, insecticide, herbicide, fungicide, pesticide. So, the quality of heated, detergent-cleansed, poison-enriched wax foundation can hardly provide the necessary environment for the bees' brood and food storage!

The second problem involves the very act of wax production; we have actually taken away from the bee its instinctive desire, need and 'right' to create its own wax!

It has become increasingly clear that many of our modern disorders and diseases in both the human and animal world can be traced to a kind of 'labor-saving' strategy that prevents the metabolic system from the very work it requires to stay healthy and productive. For example, the cow needs roughage; we humans need fibrous substances to metabolize in order to stay healthy. The intentions behind the creation of 'labor-saving' devices might be good; many of our inventions aim at saving us hard work and we are happy for it. From our human point of view it might even make sense to try and save that busy animal, the honeybee, some work. Shouldn't it be grateful for such 'kindness'? The truth, whether applied to either the human being or the bee, is that laziness or inactivity do not engender health; not working diligently results in all kind of disorders and illnesses. Persons confined to a desk job usually have to find the physical activity needed to stay healthy in an artificial way by jogging or working out in a gym. In recent times it was the astronauts who discovered this ancient truth and certainly prison administrators know or should know the physical as well as psychological benefits of a life spent in meaningful endeavor!

By supplying our bees with wax foundations for over a century, we have taken away from them not only a certain amount of work, but also a source of their vitality. We can sense what we have done to the bee most exactly when we imagine ourselves trying to save our body from constantly rebuilding our bones, which is an ongoing, extremely important process. Technically we can insert prefab bones, but it wouldn't increase our vitality walking around in prefab, recycled bones (with metal reinforcement inserted!). Some beekeepers consider it a great invention to have foundations made of synthetic material that is barely covered with a thin coating of wax. Let me not waste any words on this 'stride in progress'!

It won't be easy, but we will have to recover our reverence for the creative wisdom – which we call instinct – inherent in the animal and learn to respect basic life expressions like the metabolic activity required for bees to thrive as a vital, contributing organism, rather than just considering short–term bottom–line results. The real bottom line is ignored in our times: the frightening decrease in health and vitality in both our domesticated and many of our wild animals.

Interestingly, when the bees that *have been* subjected to wax foundations for many generations are once again allowed to build their combs with their own wax, they sometimes take two to three years to *relearn* the art of building a good comb.

Some colonies learn it faster, while others seem to have truly lost part of their wise instinct. How frightening!

If our aim is to let our honeybee regain her health and strength, then there is no doubt that we must let her create her own wax to the greatest possible extent. The denatured and chemically 'enriched' wax foundations, not to speak of the plastic foundations, have only short–term advantages for the beekeeper but do not consider the bees' intrinsic needs.

Of course we will not have the ease of honey extraction we enjoy now with wired or plastic foundations when we make the decision for natural comb. But it is possible! And a small compromise can be made to ease the transition. In new frames I attach a one-inch foundation at the top bar to give my bees some guidance in building their comb. Whenever I cut out older comb, I leave about an inch of comb at the top which usually hasn't had any brood in it. The honey extraction has to be handled more carefully, to be sure. What's the great problem if there is some breakage? The goal is anyway to let the bees build lots of new comb, an activity which contributes greatly to their health and vigor.

It all boils down to the question of whether we dare to consider the bees' own needs or only our own. The difference is vast. A healing won't be accomplished without sacrifices on our part.

*Round
straw/clay/
cow-dung
hives*

*Horizontal
hexagonal
hive built
by Tom
Wilkinson*

*Comb built
without
foundation*

The queen and her royal court

Swarm in apple tree

Beautiful white honeycomb

Drone emerging from the cell

Workers with brood, pollen, and honey

Varroa mites on honeybee larva

Busy at the round hive

Midwinter dreams

3

Queen, Workers, Drones

Human development during the past two thousand years – and especially throughout the past five hundred years – has led our culture to a predominance of specialization and segmentation in all areas of life. This has furthered the process of individualization in the human realm, and created tremendous advances in the realm of technology, both having produced many positive results.

However, there have also been negative side effects to these advancements that cannot be overlooked, for in this accelerated process we have lost our ability to interrelate different areas of life, and to think and to act in accordance with more complex laws of cause and effect. Our left hand doesn't seem to know any more what the right one is doing. But through 'surprising' environmental tragedies are we waking up, slowly enough, to the consequences of our modernized approaches; i.e., the negative impact that a dam has upon the surrounding land; the loss of humus and its connection to destructive flooding; the effects of thalidomide upon the growing embryo.

This tragic flaw of our advances in specialization must be remedied by a more integrative approach towards the interconnectedness of all living organisms in the web of life. By understanding more deeply these interrelationships, we can begin to appreciate and consider how the seemingly small or less noticeable being can play a role equally significant to an apparently larger, more influential being. For example, the Scarab Beetle is as important to the fertility of the vast stretches of prairie land in Africa as the zebra or elephant.[1] Zinc, in the dilution of 1:1 million in a lemon tree, is equally important for the ripening of the fruit as the vastly greater amounts of nitrogen, phosphorus or potassium (Pfeiffer 1983, 1:12). Whether in nutrition, medicine or ecology, in all spheres of life it is imperative that we leave the narrow and limiting emphasis on specialization and isolation and broaden our scope to include that which goes beyond our materialistic criteria of size, amount, weight and distance.

The specialization process is effective and beneficial only in the realm of technology; however, it brings forth destruction and chaos if applied to spheres of life processes. Our monoculture-agribusiness is a perfect example. When dealing with the realm of living beings we need to adapt our thinking and acting to the terms of interactive organisms, for the application of any mechanistic principles will only further disease, and ultimately, death.

Perceiving nature as a living organism will help us to more fully acknowledge the individual beings that thrive within it, and to appreciate the vital functioning of each organ as it contributes to the health of the whole. An organ – for example, a liver – has no autonomous life of its own. By itself, in isolation, it is meaningless. Yet integrated within a living being, it miraculously functions according to the laws of life governing the whole organism. Each organ within a living organism "knows" what the being needs and automatically serves this need by producing the substances in a right proportion. 'Automatically'? No, it always has to perceive the greater whole in order to be able to respond, to react correctly – in accord with all the other organs – for the benefit of the *entire organism*. These processes take place with such overwhelming complexity that it still surpasses our present-day grasp of understanding. Anyone claiming to really comprehend it all works with models of gross oversimplification.

Let us now consider the entire life expression of the bee colony. Maurice Maeterlinck, a scientist from the late nineteenth and early twentieth centuries, was still able to perceive the life of the colony as an organism and express deep awe and reverence for the greater forces and mysteries indicated by the life of the bees (Maeterlinck 1915). Modern science creates a dichotomy out of this very advanced and integrated life expression. On one hand, researchers marvel at the intricacies of activity, timing and production that the bees so amazingly execute among themselves, to provide gifts for the rest of the world (not only pollination, honey, wax). Yet under the sway of our technological mentality, they try to define the life of the bee colony by separation and delineation of its 'individual' components: queen, workers and drones.

Is it the queen, they ask, who gives the signal for new queen cells to be built, for the swarm to take leave; or do the workers initiate this process? The answer, holistically and in accordance with Maeterlinck would be: neither! The queen, workers and drones are organs themselves of the greater organism – the invisible entity that goes beyond its visible organs, which directs and controls all their activities and functions: the intelligence of a colony. Let me call it the "Spiritual Bee".

From this perspective it is now possible to take a closer look at these unique organs of this being, and try to understand more comprehensibly their purpose in context of the whole organism.

The Queen

The queen is a true ruler in the most noble sense: she is a servant her entire life. She usually mates once, high up in the air, with a number of drones, accumulating enough semen to last her for several years, producing many hundreds of thousands of offspring. On a good day in May or June, for example, she can lay several thousand eggs – a tremendous feat for her metabolism! For this task she needs special care, provided by her court of workers. She is cleaned, stroked, warmed or cooled and nourished with a special high–protein combination of pollen and honey, the royal jelly. This nourishment of highest quality enables her to transform the energy into new life at such peak performance.

Certainly the queen has an intimate and deep relationship with the workers. All of them are her progeny and she is the one that gives them the sense of belonging, the individual 'smell' of the colony. Modern beekeeping manuals suggest that a colony should be given a new queen every year, at most every two years, in order to keep up the vigor and youthfulness of the colony. From a holistic point of view this is absolute nonsense. It's a spark–plug–mentality that makes such propositions.

With the machine it is advisable to exchange a part before its efficiency decreases markedly. With a bee colony more is destroyed and interrupted through such actions than is helped. The intimate relationship of the queen to the rest of the colony,

The queen and her royal court

the aging and maturing process of such a relationship is nipped in the bud. Do we forget or have we no trust in the fact that when a queen gets old enough (four to five years) the colony will instinctively guarantee a new queen and the old one will leave on her own? Or is it our 'queen-selling business', coupled with our American dream of eternal youthfulness and abhorrence of old age that influence such a practice? No one will argue that in rare cases it is necessary to replace one queen with another one. Recent development does show, however, that a growing number of queens do not 'perform' well and *have* to be 'replaced'. But a habit of speeding up the replacement of the queens does not address, let alone solve the ills plaguing our bees.

Let me examine what in my understanding is the single most serious factor causing the lowered state of health and vitality of the honeybee: our great achievement of **artificial queen production.** This is a statement that will easily cause great discomfort, if not aggression. But hopefully a perception of inner logic and truth will be gained in the following description.

The normal course of life in the colony assures that a new queen will replace an old queen, who will leave the colony and die. If, however, a queen is accidentally killed – for example by the beekeeper while drawing frames from the hive – there usually are no queen cells in the hive to guarantee the continued life of the colony. Without a queen the entire colony would eventually die out. There is a solution for such an emergency: the workers gnaw off the six–sided cell of an egg or larva destined to become a worker bee, create a round queen cell and start feeding royal jelly. The creature resulting from this endeavor is an **'emergency queen'** – not a full–fledged one – but one who can 'fill in' until another authentic queen is raised. Usually within a year, and frequently in the same summer, a 'real' queen will quietly replace the stand–in.

We can wonder why this is so. By all physical standards the emergency queen is equal to a real queen. Yet the colony obviously is smarter than we are. Otherwise it would not replace an emergency queen so readily with an authentic one. Something must be lacking! Consider once more the power and mystery that lies behind form. In its sixteen–day development to maturity, the emergency queen has been raised for as long as four days in a hexagonal shape rather than a round one. This round form, however, creates the special environment, which, together with the specific nutritional quality, is needed for creating a *real* queen. Since all forms are also catalysts for energy fields, different cosmic forces find their expression through different forms. These energies are potent enough to become visible in the end result; the bees seem to understand this, and realize that such an emergency queen would not be suited for a long–term service to the hive.

Life does seem to need emergency solutions for unforeseen calamities. Knowing and heeding that advice, we have a spare tire in our trunk, the so–called 'doughnut', to be used for an unexpected flat tire. But nobody in his or her right mind would take this emergency tire and use it to drive from New York to San Francisco. We know that the 'real', standard–sized tire is meant to handle that task.

In beekeeping, however, we have raised the emergency queen to the level of a real queen so that currently hundreds of thousands, if not millions of queens are raised on worker–larvae, then sold and shipped all over the continent. This kind of survival solution for a colony has become the heart of queen raising for today's beekeeper. So, already, from the start, the hive begins with an emergency queen! In addition, it is currently suggested that beekeepers replenish their hives with a new queen every year or two, in order to keep the 'vigor and usefulness' of the colony. Ironically, it is this very action that prevents the aging and maturing process of the queen bee and her workers from achieving the very intimacy and strength of connection that does provide vitality, energy, resourcefulness and health! Basing our beekeeping and queen raising on such questionable practices is a dead–end street. With each successive generation we create 'built–in', inherent inferiority into our bees. On a superficial level this seems to work: we get calmer, very productive bees, bigger hives; yet inwardly the bees are less vital and increasingly prone to all kinds of virus, fungus, bacteria and parasite attacks.

We know that when the life forces that guarantee health are worn down, illness is promoted and attacks from all kind of parasites are invited. With these conditions on the rise, it is of no help to focus upon eliminating the attacker, whose job it is in nature to eradicate the weak.

In his lectures on bees, Rudolf Steiner put it this way some eighty years ago: "... much can be said for artificially breeding bees, because it does simplify quite a few things. But the strong bonding of a bee generation, a bee family, will be detrimentally affected over the longer period. But we'll have to wait and see how things will look after fifty to eighty years. Certain forces that have operated organically in the beehive until now will become mechanized; will in themselves be mechanically carried out. It won't be possible to establish the intimate relationship between a queen you have purchased and the worker bees the way it would arise all by itself in nature. But at the beginning, the effects of this are not apparent" (Steiner 1988, 21).

This industrialization and mechanization of queen raising has become the standard, at least in the Western world. Only a fast reversal of this emergency queen raising will help eradicate this calamity and will help to get the honey bee out of the emergency room. Since the raising and shipping of queens is big business in our country, a reversal will not be easy at all, to say the least!

The reversal will have to be taken up first by individuals will-ing to rely on nature's wisdom and bounty. Personal experience has proven for me as well as for many other beekeepers that the colonies are very well able to create good, productive and healthy queens. But then, I never aimed at making a business out of any aspect of beekeeping.

The Workers

The life of the queen and her workers is an inspiring tribute to the harmony and integrity that is possible for creating, sustaining and transforming life. Within one hive, for one queen, there may be as many as 50,000 to 60,000 workers during the summer. Truly the term 'labor of love' would apply to the workers, whose selfless activity is a source of marvel and amazement. The concept 'love' is not used here in the way Hollywood presents it time and again but rather in its true meaning, namely that 'love' is work; work utilizing and applying wisdom, insight, understanding. The workers' life consists of a variety of activities: they clean the cells; transport substances; alchemically change nectar to honey; feed the brood; sweat out wax; build comb; defend the hive; protect and nourish the queen; warm or cool and insulate the hive; and pollinate the flowers. They work so hard that in spring and summer their life lasts only six weeks! The first three of these weeks are spent inside on a variety of chores and the last three weeks they become forage bees, bringing home nectar, pollen, water and propolis from tree buds. They readily feed any bee that begs from them before they feed themselves. As an organ of love for the hive, these are only the most obvious tasks that the workers perform.

There is also a very significant 'micro-activity' that worker

Workers with brood, pollen, and honey

bees promote, which is to distribute a trace of the substance called formic acid (Steiner 1988, 131–138). It is the intuitive knowledge of some, but an actual fact for a few, that the formic acid produced by ants, wasps, and bees acts as a healing substance in the environment by quickening the surroundings with vitality, with life forces. For example, the forest rangers in Europe have noticed that forests die out at a faster rate when anthills are missing! They have begun restocking forests with ants as a way of restoring health to the environment. There seems to be a very important partnership of the stinging insects with the plant world. These animals do not only live off the gifts the plants provide, they also contribute their share toward health and vitality.

Although it is true that other types of bees do serve as excellent pollinators, their populations are small and their ability to create and distribute formic acid is *minute* compared to the worker honeybee. Even though the honeybee population has decreased drastically in the past twenty years (from a rough estimate of seven million colonies down to two–and–a–half million), it still provides, on the basis of sheer numbers, the most extensive creation and distribution of formic acid within our ecosystem.

This formic acid distribution and its effect upon vegetation is yet another reason to appreciate, protect and encourage the health and vitality of our honey bees so they may continue to serve the plant world in this rather mysteriously hidden, revitalizing activity. Since the relationship between plants and the human being represents the greatest and most basic symbiosis in relation to breathing, this benefit certainly reaches our lives and of course, affects the life and health of all other animals.

A myriad of factors come together to reduce the workers' vitality. The beekeeper's attitude, which determines the methods applied, is but one side of the coin. The array of environmentally damaging influences of our time – monocultures, artificial fertilizers, genetically modified plants, pesticides and insecticides, crass reduction of wild flowers, water and air pollution, micro– and macrowaves, reduced ozone – all these and more present a problem even to the best–intentioned beekeeper.

One problem that can easily be avoided is the carelessness, yes, sometimes even the brutality with which workers are treated by their 'keepers': transported time and again long distances, chased away with chemicals, blown or vacuumed; or simply torn apart from their organism at times when it is like surgery for the colony (we'll mention later a more appropriate time when a split can be made).

If you acquire a deep gratitude and reverence for your bees, you will gently warn them of your intrusion with a puff of smoke, perhaps even a kind word of greeting. Normally you won't need gloves or a suit, probably not even a veil when you work your bees, even when you collect some honey. We don't own a suit and veil, and our gloves are collecting dust. All suited up, you will tend to go *at* the bees rather than *to* them and they will react accordingly. In later chapters we will consider other factors beside the ones discussed which affect the workers' well-being.

The Drones

After looking into the life expression of the queen bee and the worker bees, let us complete the picture by observing the drones.

These plump, amiable, gentle males are physically the largest and heaviest of the three kinds of bees in the hive. They have much larger feelers and much larger eyes than the workers; you can even hold them in your hand and they won't sting you since they have no 'weapon' at all! Their very distinguished important role within the hive seems to be limited to mating with the queen. And not all of them; only a few will perform that task. They are almost the opposite of worker bees: they don't work at all, they can't even feed themselves; the workers feed them. To an observer they play a very passive role among all the 'busy bees' until the 'right' sunny day. Then they fly up about 500–600 feet into the air, hovering in mysterious locations that attract drones from a radius as wide as eight to ten miles. The young queens fly up to these 'meadows in the sky', up and beyond the cloud of drones, followed by the lightest and strongest of them. Up to a dozen can mate with the queen – and die. The queen returns to the hive with enough semen to normally last her a lifetime, four to five years.

Drones are, without doubt, vital to the propagation of the hive. However, let's look again at the essence of this being that has such pronounced eyes and feelers and take a look beyond its reproductive role. If we think again about organs, what organs in our body don't play an outwardly active role; don't really visibly work as our muscles do, have a minimum of metabolic activity? What organs more or less 'take in' most of their lives? In our body it is the sense organs that seem to be so passive, just calmly and quietly perceiving, sensing. And yet they are the organs which unite us with the outer world, letting us experience communion with the substances, sounds, colors of the world, passing on to the rest of the body the quality that is out there in the light, the food, the smells, the music and language. Through analogy, we can certainly conceive of the drone as an organ of perception, but perception for what?

Could we take an even larger step into the realm of the Spiritual Bee, the invisible being that guides all life expressions, all activities of the physical colony, no matter where they live? Rudolf Steiner called such beings the Group Soul. The wisdom that emanates from this being we simply refer to as instinct, which does not, as we might be tempted to believe, originate in the genes. We would rather have to consider the genes to be the tools of this invisible being for the performance of multitudes of functions particular to a specific animal: the bees, the lions, the horses, and so forth.

If we can hypothetically assume a greater being, of which each colony is but one physical representative, then it is possible to intuit that the drones serve as specific sense organs of the colony for this group soul, especially at the height of activity cresting between May and July. However, such a function is never only a one-way street; the opposite is also true: the group soul perceives the colony strongly – not exclusively – through the drones in the period of propagation, reproduction. Such an image takes one beyond the question of 'who' decides the building of swarm cells, the creation of new queens, the swarming of the old queen. Of course it is neither the workers, nor the queen, not even to mention the drones. It is the invisible Spiritual Bee that works with wisdom in all organs of the colony.

What do we actually achieve by manipulating the colonies so as to have less and less drones by cutting out drone brood, or by means of prefab foundations, which limit the bees to raising workers? Are we creating a sensory deprivation, 'blinding' the bee colony, making it 'deaf and dumb' by attempting to control the number of drones?

In the figure on the next page, we can look at the life span of the drone within the yearly cycle of the hive, enhancing in a picturesque way the understanding of the drones as sense organs.[1]

For quite a few beekeepers the drones are lazy, superfluous feeders that have to be limited for the sake of more honey and worker brood. These individuals must assume that if they can't detect a meaning, there is none; and Mother Nature simply made a mistake. For most contemporary beekeepers, all efforts are geared to achieving greater efficiency of bee labor and increased honey production, and this means in clear text that fewer 'superfluous' feeders, i.e., drones, are desired. The practice of cutting out drone brood and limiting it with worker cell foundations is advocated in many bee manuals.

Doesn't it raise questions that in spite of our smartness and inventiveness we are losing the honeybee, and not her alone?

Is it possible to perceive what happens when we lose respect and reverence for the beings of nature who inherently thrive upon their own rhythm and harmonious interrelationship with each other and the surrounding natural forces?

As stewards of this earth we certainly are called upon to become co-creators, not just to leave nature as it has been created. We have ennobled grasses into grains, created beautiful landscapes, and have introduced culture into nature as our human contribution. Up until very recent times these changes were achieved with the aid of deep wisdom of the creative forces of the cosmos, out of a deep reverence and love for creation.

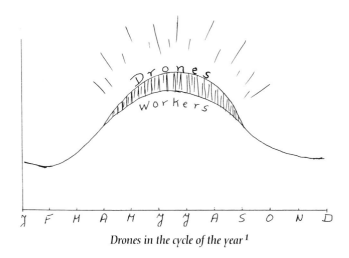

Drones in the cycle of the year [1]

Drone emerging from the cell

These qualities seem to be lacking more and more, and our motives, not only our senses, have become impoverished. Now we let the microscope and the stock market, not the cosmos and ideals, dictate our actions: we want to save time, money, effort and discomfort; and we sow seeds of disharmony, illness and ultimately death. Perhaps it is not too late to re-evaluate many of the modern approaches to beekeeping that are so threatening to the integrity of life in the hive. Can we embrace once more, with reverence and awareness, those processes that appear to be outmoded or old-fashioned but which are, in their very nature, the keys to the wisdom and miraculous quality of our natural world?

1) Wolfgang Schad, from a lecture given in Dornach, Switzerland circa 1988.
2) From a lecture by the German farmer Mannteufel.

4

Swarming

People who have found themselves in the midst of a mighty swarm or who has observed this incredible act from a distance cannot help but admit that the experience itself evokes rather indescribable thoughts and emotions. Swarming is a powerful and vibrant expression of a healthy, well-functioning bee colony. It is at once mysterious, lucid and transcendent. Swarming supersedes, by its very display and magnitude, all that is commonplace, 'status quo' and subdued in our everyday human activity. We may discover upon closer examination why swarming is so intrinsic to the bee's physical and spiritual health.

The springtime environment perfectly supports the physical growth of the colony. When the sun reaches a certain height in February, the queen starts laying eggs even though the outside temperatures may still be chilling. By May the colony has built up its numbers tremendously and the flow of nectar from mother nature's bounty has filled the combs with that most delicate of substances – worked on and ennobled by the bees' diligence, enriched with enzymes and ferments, resulting in that delicious miracle: honey. In addition, a good amount of pollen is also stored. This surplus of spring honey and pollen guarantees the continuity of raising brood in leaner summer months; these are reserves for rainy periods or when the nectar flow ebbs down. It is at this time, then, that the hive is a land of plenty, abundant with honeycomb, which was mostly built during the previous year, abounding in brood and food. Opening a hive at this time gives one the impression that all is well!

Such is the physical condition that sets the stage for the swarm. Now a demonstration of their sublime instincts and social organization begins to unfold.

It is at the peak of fruition, when the hive is filled with provisions, when there is no room to continue to work vigorously with diligence and joy, that the workers start to create a number of round cells in which the queen lays her eggs, so that a new queen may enter into existence. A few days later, a loosening of the bonds uniting the entire colony can be observed. The workers who have been diligently collecting nectar, pollen, water, and propolis begin to slow down; the worker's latent ovaries begin to develop; and a general mood of relaxation and waiting – not to say laziness – prevails in the colony.[1]

A few days before the new queen (usually more than one) emerges from her cell, on a fair day in the late morning, the old queen and approximately one half of the workers, as well as a number of drones, leave their beloved hive: the swarming begins! Like a pot of soup boiling over, masses of bees pour out of the hive entrance in a continuing stream. The entire swarm, led by the old queen, creates a loose vortex – a living tornado – humming and swiftly spiraling anywhere from eight to twenty-five feet high! What a stunning sight to see a mass of 10–30,000 bees flying at great speed, describing a sphere of thirty to forty feet, never bumping into or intruding upon one another! This moving globe of insects continues until the queen chooses a place to land. The circle draws tighter, with the swarm hanging on a branch, growing more and more massive, until the entire swarm congregates into a shape resembling a huge, ripe plum. Next, the 'scouts' start to fly in search of a new home. If nothing appropriate is found within a few hours, the swarm will normally take to the air once more and fly a few miles to settle yet again in a tree. The future is open, the outcome of this venture unknown. Will they find a cavity in a tree or inside a protected cave, or will they use up their reserves, which will last for approximately three days?

As frightening as such an act of swarming appears to the uninitiated, the swarm bees are gentle bees. It is possible to put your hand into the 'plum' hanging from a branch without being stung. It is as if they have something more important to do, which requires complete focus and attention.

At this point, we can begin to appreciate the spiritual nature of such a magnificent phenomenon. First of all, the act of leaving one's home at the point of highest productivity and achievement, leaving the fruits of their work to another is a true sacrifice and demonstration of love from our human point of view. It is similar to a situation where the house is built, the furniture is in place, the bank account has a nice reserve, and the time has come for retirement and recreation. The natural inclination would be to settle down in comfort and luxury for the remaining years of one's life. Not so for the bees! Swarming is the very antithesis of the desire to sink into comfort. The bees demonstrate through swarming a reversal of this human inclination, and would no doubt inspire the following scenario. Just imagine Pa telling Ma,

"Isn't it nice what we have accomplished? Yet somehow I feel that if we take it easy and relax too much, we will stop developing our human potential to the fullest. Why don't we leave all of this to the children? They will be blessed and challenged with our gift and will surely not use up, but further develop, all that they have received from us. Let's take a modest amount out of our bank account and move on. Let's see if we can find ourselves a new place where we can begin building once again. You know, I feel that I am only true to my life's purpose when I live in creative activity." And Ma's eyes would light up and she would say: "You are right, my love. Let's go."

A German mother would add: "Ja, Arbeit macht das Leben suess." (It's work that makes life sweet.) And then off they would go, leaving their life's bounty to the young ones, not knowing what they themselves would encounter, with no guarantee that they would even succeed in their bold adventure.

Most of us would feel that this decision was crazy. Who would want to take such risks and relinquish so much security after so much work? Few would be willing to make this leap of faith. Yet anyone who by fate and circumstance has been in the position to make such a step knows what an invigorating, rejuvenating quality enters one's life as a result. No insurance company can offer such benefits.

As if the act of swarming was not glorious enough, there is another sequel to this dramatic unfolding. For the bees either find a shelter where they can build up a new colony, or they die. However, when the beekeeper captures the swarm, he puts it into a box and stores it in a cool, dark, quiet cellar overnight.

Beautiful white honeycomb

In the late afternoon of the next day, he places them into the newly appointed hive box. Within only a few days of residing in their new location, the bees produce something phenomenal: they produce the most beautiful white honeycomb with a diligence greater than any other time! It is awe-inspiring to pick up some of the translucent, little wax plates that the workers 'sweat' out of their abdomen, and which are sometimes dropped in the activity of building the cells. They harden quickly and can't be used by the building team. They remind me of tiny clear lenses or bits of clear mountain crystal. There must be thousands used for one cell alone. What a feat!

From this spectacular show of transformation, we can see another powerful principle at work in swarming, as one travels the cycle from a state of form (hive) to chaos (swarm) to a new state of form (new hive). It can be compared to the cycle we experience daily, from wakefulness (form) to sleep (unconsciousness or chaos) back to a new awakening and its formed activity. It is precisely out of this state of sleep, of relative formlessness, that we are renewed, refreshed and invigorated. In a similar way, the swarm leaves the honeycombs, which were formed out of instinctual wisdom, brought to fruition by social activity, (representing wakefulness and the result of higher consciousness); and proceeds once more into an unformed state of chaos (a kind of dreamy formlessness and sleep) in the act of swarming. This newly created chaos, in its absence of form, houses a great promise, a flourishing, energizing potential, from which a newly formed comb structure can emerge.

Does this reflection upon swarming activity help to clarify why swarming is one of the most rejuvenating, revitalizing activities in the life cycle of the honeybee? (Steiner 1998, 156) Why it should be furthered rather than thwarted? It is as revitalizing as waking up after a good night's sleep. Imagine if we had no sleep, no 'escape' from the perpetual, conscious, form-driven activity of the day, because it would waste time, productivity and money. Would we not be drained of our life forces very quickly, weaken our immune system, become ill and die? Why then, would this not be true for the bee as well?

How many of these fundamental, vitally important activities can we take away from our bees, expecting them to reduce their lives to honey production for profit? The swarming activity itself is pivotal for the right functioning of queens, workers and drones, for the organically correct activity of *naturally* raised queens.

It is amazing how many methods have been created during the past one hundred years to prevent bees from swarming. Fortunately, these attempts are often defeated by the stronger, overpowering forces of what we call instinct. We must begin to again acknowledge the wisdom inherent in instinct, for the basic instincts in nature's kingdoms all pertain to the will and ability to survive and thrive.

There are factors beyond technological thinking and profit-making strategies that suggest the need to curb swarming. One of those is the beginning and subsequent dramatic rise in professional beekeeping. Formerly bees were part of the farm organism; pastors and teachers kept a few hives in their back yards; swarms could be captured easily. The ones that weren't captured flew freely to the woodlands and established feral colonies. Currently, most professional beekeepers live a fair distance away from their hives, so the bees cannot be monitored as easily. In this circumstance one could view swarming as a nuisance to uninformed and frightened neighbors and as a loss; if the colony flies away, so does some of the honey. One can also sympathize with the frustration of losing a colony, regardless of the profits!

So if the beekeeper is confronted with the choice to prevent swarm activity or to give up beekeeping entirely, then probably keeping bees as respectfully as possible is a more important course of action. In the situation where swarming cannot be allowed, the development of the colony can be monitored and, at the right time, a split can be made; certainly a compromise. A beekeeper can check the hives from late April into June to determine if new queens are being raised. The ideal time for splitting the hive 'artificially' rather than by swarms is when the first queen cell is just capped. This is the time when the unity in the hive is broken, and the workers either begin to align themselves with the new queen, or remain in service to the old queen. At this time, the colony can be divided into two, perhaps even three colonies (if the original colony is very strong), one with the old queen and the other with young queens. Such a split is like a

Swarm in apple tree

'minor surgery' that can be accommodated within the organic processes of the hive, rather than a more traumatizing 'major surgery', which happens when the colony is split arbitrarily at times when the bonds have not been loosened.

Interestingly, Africanized bees, which are still full of vigor and vitality since we have not manipulated them, seem to have a powerful instinct for swarming; they do so incessantly! This type of bee represents the complete opposite of what we have tried to breed and have raised to our ideal: a very placid bee who is reluctant to swarm.

I am convinced that bees should be allowed to swarm, that we should not suppress their basic instinct, for swarming represents the innate wisdom that lives within and around their entire sphere of life expression. Swarming will no doubt contribute significantly to raising the bee's natural health and resistance to all kind of fungal, bacterial, and parasitic attacks. Nature, with her instinctual wisdom, 'knows' and produces long-lasting, beneficial effects. The environmental crises of our century speak a clear language.

Let us pause in our fast pace of questionable achievements, take inventory and an honest look at the consequences of our thoughts and deeds and let us listen anew to what nature can tell us when we open not only our eyes, but also our hearts!

---

1) Thomas Radetzki, from an oral presentation at a workshop at the Verein fuer Wesensgemaesse Bienenhaltung, Rosenfeld, Germany, 1994.

43

5

Honey and Pollen

The beneficial and healing properties of honey and pollen for the human being are statistically proven (Herold 1970). One thing is sure: honey is much more than a substitute for any other sweetener.

As we begin to comprehend more deeply the nature of the honeybee and all that surrounds and inspires her life, it should be no surprise that honey and pollen, which serve as the sole source of nourishment for these creatures, are some of the most delicate, rarefied, and miraculous substances in all of nature. They provide, in chemically varying mixtures combined with added enzymes, ferments, hormones and trace minerals, the liquid food for larvae and sustain the adult bees throughout their entire life. Honey and pollen continually sustain the bees throughout their entire life.

What is it about these substances that make them so unique? What makes the honey more appropriate for the bee's nourishment than any type of sugar? And pollen! Is it not that precarious, unappreciated powder that gives many people seasons of sneezing, wheezing and coughs?

When we study the process of photosynthesis, we can see that sugars are created in the leaf of the plant. They are, in one form or another, the original primary nutrient for all living beings on this earth. They provide the chemical foundation for the creation of carbohydrates, proteins, fats and cellulose within the plant. In the process of photosynthesis, water, oxygen, carbon and nitrogen – all of which don't really taste good in their pure form – synthesize with sunlight, and combine with this life–giving stream. Lo and behold: the result tastes great!! These enlivened substances, refined by Nature's own processing, are now filtered up to the flower of a plant to create nectar, which along with the fragrant etheric oils, is the culmination of the plant's delicate substances. The sweetness is so subtle that we can only taste it in a few plants, such as honeysuckle and lilac.

Pollen is also a very delicate substance, one that is created from the plant by the Sun's light *and* warmth. It is high in protein and very stable (still found in Egyptian graves), and yet it is light enough to be released into the higher altitudes, where it circles the atmosphere of the earth.

Such mysterious, marvelous substances are the bee's life sustaining nourishment. Yet, to our rather indiscriminate sense for quality differences, sugar is sugar and protein is protein! So why not take as much honey from the hive as possible and give the bees sugar syrup for the winter and early spring? It is simply a fact that neither cane sugar nor beet sugar is suitable for the bee's metabolic, digestive processes (Steiner 1998, 38). Whereas the plant's nectar is an entity in itself, a 'complete food', the sugar we buy is a fragment, a substance that was isolated, separated from a plant's organ, either the root or stalk. *The strain of converting mineralized sugar into a simulation of honey is an exhausting, depleting and nutritionally depriving activity for the bees.* In human nutrition we now know that sugar robs the body of essential minerals, trace minerals in the process of digestion. It yearns to be 'whole' again. Why do we assume that the honeybee suffers no negative effects from being fed sugar?

We put on a similar scenario with the pollen. Why not give the bee colony a pollen substitute in early spring in order to accelerate the brood production? Let's be clear about this: what we consider to be a substitute for pollen is very far from even approaching this fine substance, because it is generally derived from soybeans! Again, one has to say that protein is not 'just' protein. The soybean product is a much coarser, denser substance than what is created in the flower of a plant. The source makes all the difference.

If we as humans were given grass or tree bark as food, would our digestive system adjust readily to this substitute? Perhaps in an absolute crisis we could survive on it for a short time, but not for a longer period. Even if the same elements lived within the coarser food, weakness, discomfort, illness and death would result. Of course, this is a drastic comparison. In the case of

Frame of capped honey

sugar feeding, factors undermining the health and vitality of the bee are subtler and take longer to show effects. I believe that we are witnessing the results of more than a century of harm but are not making the right diagnosis. For the bees' poor health we still put the blame on bacteria, viruses and mites, rather than looking at the deficiency of our conventional practices.

It is our ignorance and lack of sensitivity that play a part, no doubt. Our perception and thinking need to be trained anew, in order to perceive subtle differences of quality and their unique effect on living organisms. If financial gain remains our main motive then we can be certain that rich fathers will leave behind poor sons!

Honey and pollen, including the invaluable service of pollinating approximately three-fourths of the produce we eat, are a true blessing for mankind. With this in mind, with the sense of deep gratitude and of awe, we can reflect upon the respect and the care that was given to the bees' own rights and needs in the past. Until the late nineteenth century, only surplus honey was taken from the colony. What was considered surplus? Whatever was in the hive from the previous year at the time when, for example, the dandelion was in bloom and the new supply of forage was steady. With the orchards flowering soon thereafter, one knew that the 'old' honey was no longer needed by the colony for its survival and well-being. No substitutes were given in order to be able to take more from them.

Could we find a reasonable way of handling this situation again? I do take some honey in June from the hives that have gathered a great surplus. But I leave them enough to be able to cope with a poor honey flow or a wet summer. In addition, I keep a reserve of honey in case there is not enough in a hive to take them through the winter. Only on rare occasions do I mix some sugar with honey and a mild herb tea made with chamomile, sage, and a pinch of salt, to reduce the strain on their metabolism. In middle to late April, when the dandelion starts to bloom, I will then take most, not all, of the surplus honey. This is one of their gifts for our own health and well-being. They will thrive with an adequate supply of their own rightful sustenance, and we will evolve from the degrading role of exploiter to the fulfilling honor of being a steward.

6

Health, Parasites,
Diseases, and Treatments

Health is a difficult concept to define. When we are healthy, we at best acknowledge it in a relaxed, almost presumptuous way. We have a rather dreamy and unconscious attitude toward the automatic functioning of our bodies. We live unaware, for the most part, of the perfect interrelationships of our organs, tissues, cells and fibers to the liquids, warmth and air that balance us so beautifully toward a state of being that we can experience and appreciate as health. We most often don't wake up to health until it is lacking, when our organism is somehow distressed or imbalanced. And we seldom address the nature of illness or imbalance until we acquire one of such fortitude that it forces us to spend time, money and pay attention.

Let us reflect upon the physical, emotional and spiritual factors that may contribute to discomfort, disease, or a general lack of health in a living organism. On a physical level, an organism may be affected by wounds; by the entry of a foreign substance or living being (bacteria or virus); or by environmental, atmospheric pollution that causes a poisoning or otherwise overwhelms the physical integrity and immunity of the organism.

Psychological distress of a mental or emotional nature can also result in physical difficulty. Prevailing habitual negative emotions and thoughts can eventually wreak havoc upon the body, creating physical damage or illness. The soul (psyche) has its effects on the body (soma), resulting in psychosomatic illnesses, as psychiatrists and physicians witness daily. We have all experienced throughout our own lives the physical reactions of our bodies to the emotional peaks of joy and suffering.

The spiritual causes of illness, though elusive, are probably the most pervasive ones, even though rarely diagnosed as such. When we are, from our innermost being, in tune with the creative forces and beings of our universe, then we are able to overcome those obstacles and handicaps that occur on the psychological and physical levels. In some instances, we can really move mountains! If, however, we have cut ourselves off completely from this powerful spiritual source within us, we tend to lose touch with our highest ideals and those guiding thoughts and actions that ennoble us to rise above our daily worries and tasks. When this happens, we lose the true appreciation of ourselves and the world around us: we tend to lose at least part of the deep reverence, awe and wonder that arises from a spiritual view of this world as part of an entire cosmic creation. As a result, our physical organism is weakened, we become less resilient and more vulnerable, since we have separated ourselves from our spiritual origin. We are lacking wholeness. The word 'whole' is actually related to the words 'heal' as well as 'holy'. No wonder that presently one can witness a deep yearning, a true striving toward healing, toward holistic thinking and doing. It's a vital, necessary reaction against the paradigm still ruling, which reduces and fractures into isolated components that which is whole.

Our modern, materialistic society operates with a 'fix–it–quick', 'the–most–obvious–culprit–is–the–cause' type of attitude. It is this impoverished 'Weltanschauung' that has drastically reduced our rightful, authentic understanding of life and life processes (Steiner 1994, chap. 1) This has, in turn, thwarted our relationship to nature so that it is now one of exploitation rather than true awareness and stewardship. If we can step out of our presently dominant paradigm long enough to look at the entire picture (the Gestalt) of human, animal and plant life, it may be possible to relate to the concepts of health and disease in a more conscious, sensitive way. We may come to realize the incredible importance of vitality and well–being for the healthy functioning of any living organism.

Most of us are aware of the brutal ways that we keep and treat cows, chickens and pigs. Pictures of industrialized farms can be seen in the media, where 26,000 chickens a year are 'produced' in tiny coops; pig farms where 2,000 pigs or more are imprisoned in stalls that are so small that the sows can't even turn around; cattle 'factories' where the thousands of dull–eyed bulls spend their lives tied down, never catching a glimpse of the blue sky or the green pasture. But we, as consumers, seem to have blocked all of their suffering out of our consciousness because the price is right, i.e. cheap. Does it occur to many people that we also consume their suffering, not only their meat; that it is a sin against these friends and benefactors of human evolution; that we are to be their stewards, not their torturers?

The word 'animal' is a derivative of the Greek word *anima*, which also means 'soul'. An animal is a living being endowed with a soul! In other words, it has the ability to move and feel, to have motion and emotion. If we could experience an animal's language, what do you think a chicken, in one of those tiny mesh cages, would tell us about her being reduced to an egg–laying or meat–producing entity? Is it any wonder that the life expectancy of cows has dropped from twenty–five or more years to six or seven years; that some chickens can no longer hatch their own eggs; that our domesticated animals' fertility and innate life forces have decreased to a frightening extent, their susceptibility to disease sharply risen due to our greed, neglect or plain stupidity. We have demonstrated a regrettable inability to create for these animals anything resembling a healthy environment.

Are we really surprised, considering the extreme manipulation of hives, food, swarming, queen raising, nutritional and medici-

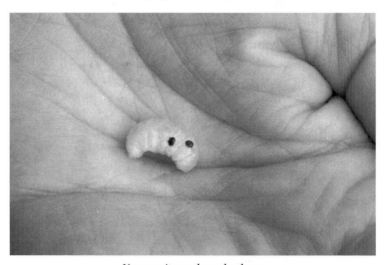

Varroa mites on honeybee larva

nal intrusions, that the bee colonies themselves have diminished in the USA from approximately seven million to little more than two million in just twenty years? [1]

Herein we can see the interplay of physical, emotional and spiritual factors that so urgently need to be addressed in our treatment of animals. And it is from this point of view that we can look again at the role of parasites and diseases that plague our bees.

Varroa and tracheal mites, as well as foulbrood, are among the predominant killers of today's honeybee population. Beekeepers designate the varroa mite as the number one enemy, and suggest basically two ways of eradicating these destructive creatures and their 'associates':

- to breed a bee, perhaps even through bio-engineering, that is resistant to varroa and tracheal mites;
- to simply 'wipe out' these aggressors with chemicals developed by pesticide and pharmaceutical companies.

In the first instance, we know that whenever a new breed is created as a way of avoidance or suppression of some external force, yet another unsuspected and undesired weakness inherent to the new breed invariably appears. Anyone familiar with the development of hybrids in the plant world knows that the new, desirable traits achieved invariably bring along others that pose new challenges; challenges that are not necessarily easier to solve in the long-run than what we tried to overcome. Secondly, several of the chemicals sold on the market as treatment have already begun to lose their effectiveness. We should have

Varroa mites

learned our lessons well from DDT and similar hazardous chemical experiments! (Carson 1962)

It is our societal attitude and generally accepted theory that the symptoms (i.e., bacteria or virus) are the cause of the disease. Perhaps this is only partially true, if at all. Suppose we consider these health-threatening parasites and bacteria as *indicators* – but not the causes – of disease among the bees. If we look at the word 'dis-ease' it says that a living being itself is not 'at ease'.[2] It is not functioning with enough strength to ward off 'invaders'. If the parasites and bacteria themselves were really the *cause* of so much illness, then why – and how – has the Far Eastern honey-bee been able to survive the varroa mite for centuries, perhaps millennia? Its natural vitality lets it cope with the parasite by means of diligent swarm habits; and also by grooming off and even biting the intruder! The honeybee of the Far East has remained healthy! We know from our own experience that we become resourceful in dealing with attacks on our being, whether physical or psychological, when we are really fit, vibrant and healthy. When depressed, exhausted or otherwise 'down and under', we easily become victim to any kind of attack, whether of a physical (i.e., bacteria, viruses or parasites) or emotional type.

The nature of a parasite is defined by a one-sided relationship: only one party benefits from the encounter. This is relatively rare in nature, for most relationships are symbiotic; in other words, both parties benefit. However, an important factor that is often missed with regard to a parasite is that if it kills off the host completely, it too is doomed to perish. Thus a 'wise' parasite never wipes out its source of life completely. And so, in a sense, the very fact that the varroa and tracheal mites successfully attack so many bees is a signal to both species that there is life-threatening danger and imbalance!

If we look at the human world and actually believe the germ theory to be true (i.e., that the germ or virus is the real cause of the illness), then doctors and nurses should be constantly ill, due to their exposure to so many viruses, bacteria and germs. Yet this is not the case! What protects them? It cannot be hygienic practices only, for there were doctors and nurses *before* these new 'precautionary measures' were invented. It is most likely that their general attitude, idealism and inner strength allow them to remain in good health amidst the sick patients to whom they are dedicated.

One can look at the plant world as well, through the work of the gardener. The seed once planted does not germinate automatically. All the necessary conditions must be present, such as warmth or frost; moisture; the appropriate amount of light or darkness. If these environmental criteria are not met, the seed may lie in the ground for years – decades or longer – until the 'perfect growing conditions' arise. What we have generally forgotten is the all-decisive factor of **context** (Holdrege 1996). There are absolutely no automatic cause–effect relationships between parasite, virus, and bacterium on the one side, and illness on the other. Inner readiness is the most important single criterion. This explains why a great number of individuals can be exposed to a certain virus or bacterium and only a fraction of the persons 'catch' the illness.

In the case of our honeybee, both the question and quest lie in finding out what the real causes of this critical readiness are. Suppose that mites and foulbrood are just the symptoms – not the causes – of the imbalance threatening the distressed and dying bees. Suppose they enter their bodies more easily because the bees themselves lack vigor, vitality or 'joie de vivre'. They are too weak to offer any resistance. They have no resilience left for a good fight! Of course we can spend a lot of time and money trying to breed a resistant bee through bio-engineering, or to develop all kinds of drugs to eliminate aggressors. These venues will not tackle the real problem; they will not give back health and vitality to our bees. These attempts will merely lure us from one short-lived illusionary success to the next one. In the meantime the real cause has not been confronted and dealt with at all!

Let's face it: if we wipe out the parasites, the foulbrood spores, the intestinal bacteria, then we will have only postponed looking for the real causes. No lasting solution will be obtained. The next fatal enemy will appear on stage. In fact, it has! This new enemy now appears in the form of the Hive Beetle. Imported from Africa, this beetle is presently destroying colonies in the South of the US but is also steadily moving up North. We can discover the same phenomenon in the human realm. We wipe out polio, scarlet fever, and the plague, only to have them replaced by the arrival of HIV, Epstein–Barr virus, Lyme disease, and West Nile

Virus. Instead of gratefully looking at *symptoms* of illness as *warning* signals trying to tell us of deeper lying causes, we tend to fight the signals, not heeding their message to wake up.

The generally accepted theory that bacteria or viruses are the *cause of disease* is still, unfortunately, the prevalent one in our society. Understanding that the more important factor involved is the general state of health and the ability of the immune system to ward off attacks, is a truth that was once known but for the past few centuries has been ever more forgotten and neglected. Very slowly but surely this insight is making its way even into the ranks of modern scientists. Anita Collins, a research geneticist at the Agriculture Department's Bee Research Laboratory in Beltsville, Md., writes: "If you have a strong bee colony, and they're healthy, they would probably keep these critters under control (here she refers to the attack of the African Hive Beetle). If you've got a weaker colony, then these beetles can sort of get out of hand." (Anderson 7/7/98)

Treatments

What can we do? Are there any remedies that may be more environmentally compatible, ones that can lead us to a positive footing on the path for a new foundation for our ailing bees? Are there any temporary measures to be used in the interim of a major 'environmental and beekeeping overhaul' towards the renewed health and vitality of the bees?

One suggested remedy is the use of *natural oils* to keep the mites in check. This is not, in my opinion, a good solution, although it is appealing in a sensory way. The fact that oils don't evaporate readily means that they accumulate in the honey and wax. The long term effects of these residues on the bees is unknown – which means that it is not yet safe to use them. Their effectiveness, although noted in a few cases, is by no means proven in broader and long-range trials.

There are, however, two provisional treatments that are able to minimize – and some cases eradicate – varroa and tracheal mites to a significant degree. These treatments involve the use of two common acids, *formic acid and oxalic acid.* These substances, according to Rudolf Steiner, are very essential in all life processes and are present in fine dilutions not only in the bee colony, but also in all of nature (Steiner 1998, Lectures 7 & 8).

Formic acid and oxalic acid were, to my knowledge, first introduced in Germany by a group of beekeepers whose aim is to heal and rejuvenate the honeybee population through scientific knowledge, environmental awareness, and spiritual insight into the true nature of the honeybee.[3] They have been using treatments that support and enhance the basic health and immune system of the bees themselves, rather than resorting to antidotes that are harsh and artificial. Their acid treatments have been by tested by the Entomology Department of the Agricultural University of Hohenheim in Stuttgart, Germany and other institutes in Europe (Liebig 1999). At this point both treatments – as well as variations by other practitioners – are described and evaluated in public bee journals and ways are sought to simplify and standardize these treatments to guarantee effectiveness as well as safety for the beekeeper (ADIZ 2000, 11:9–11). (See Appendix A for description of these treatments).

Whereas formic acid has been permitted for use in this country since 1999, oxalic acid treatment is relatively unknown. Both acids have been tested and no residue has been found in honey or wax in all tests. Scientific research suggests the prognosis that the use of these acids will *not* cause the mites to build resistance or immunity to these substances over the years.

Another potential alternative may be the use of lactic acid. This possibility has been used by some beekeepers in Europe, but has not been sufficiently investigated through systematic research or experimentation. It is certainly worth exploring. When we consider all the beneficial substances given to us by the cow in the form of dairy products and also through the great fertility of its dung, perhaps its lactic acid as well may provide a healing or rejuvenating element for the bee. Perhaps 'the land of milk and honey' is not only a metaphor, but also a potential reality that supports renewed strength and vigor. This may be yet another example of the interrelationships of living beings, and the way they support and heal one another in the web of life.

Nevertheless, we must realize that none of these suggested treatments for the control of mites are the ultimate solution; rather, they are temporary measures to help the bees survive until they re–establish their full vigor and immunity to external irritants and to the environmental stress that surrounds them.

Foulbrood is a disease that is traced to the bacillus larvae in strictly medical terms; yet again, if we look at the holistic environment it is apparent that there are many contributing factors that facilitate this modern ailment afflicting so many bees.

Since foulbrood affects the brood rather than the adult bee, it is appropriate to examine the conditions that surround the queen, as well as the nourishment the brood receives. The queen is fed a substantial amount of high protein food, which is responsible for invigorating her metabolism to such an extent that she is able to lay an enormous number of eggs each day (up to 1500, according to some statistics). Now we must ask if this food she receives is of a good quality. There are many environmental pollutants and poisons affecting the food supply in general today; over ninety percent of our food plants are grown with mineral fertilizers, resulting in weakened plants in need of external protection.

In addition, the sugar and pollen substitutes that are fed to the bees instead of leaving them enough fruits of their own labor result in something that approaches honey but is of inferior quality, as any chemist will tell you. We know that eating a lot of sugar disturbs the stomach, causing increased acidity. The bee's blood is alkaline; so with the sugar feeding the delicate balance of alkalinity is upset. Converting sugar into some sort of honey is a burdensome task for the worker bees; it strains their metabolic system, as mentioned before. This 'honey', together with the pollen substitutes, is then part of the food used in raising the brood as well as feeding the queen. Delicate biochemical relationships are upset, such as the relationship between the gastric juices and the blood, one being acid, the other alkaline (Steiner 1998, 86–87).

We may safely assume, then, that the food that the queen and the brood receive, is not nutritionally sound, and therefore does not provide the balance and vitality for their optimum health. This deficiency results, on the one hand, in eggs that are not as healthy and vibrant as they should be; and, on the other hand, in larvae that are nourished with inferior products. It is at this point that nature wants to help by getting rid of weakness and inferiority. As a result of these conditions, the means – and not the cause – is the foulbrood bacillus!

Nature can be relied upon to provide us with visible, tangible symptoms that show us an underlying problem. The wise farmer knows that thistles show the spots that have a condensed, an impenetrable layer in the subsoil. The thistles with their powerful taproots try to correct this 'illness' of the soil. The farmer, in response, will either let the thistles do the work; or he may sow lupines to help with the problem; or he may use a chisel plow to break up the dense stratum of soil. Only the stupid farmer will condemn the patch of thistles and use an herbicide to get rid of them. He will wipe out the indication that something is wrong underneath, but, unfortunately, he will not have solved the problem.

The message of the mites and the foulbrood is a similar one. We will not have achieved anything if we can wipe out these 'culprits'. We have to get at the root of the problems they present to us in order to solve them. And that means that we have to change all that has contributed to creating the problem in the first place. As previously explained, one of the major factors undermining the queen's health is related to the modern achievement of raising queens. For over one hundred years, the 'emergency queen' has supplanted the truly natural, authentic queen that was the tradition of healthy bees for millennia. This stress-inducing, inferior way of breeding has definitely been detrimental to the blood and metabolism of queens in general. Inferiority has been bred into the hives without our intending to do so or becoming aware of detrimental effects. A growing number of reports about failing queens, about queens not lasting longer than a few months, give a clear indication about the seriousness of the situation.

Holistically and intuitively we know what we have to do. But a development that has taken more than a century to reach this state of crisis will not be changed overnight. The healing process will take time.

One way to help raise the health and vitality of the colony is to offer the bees an herb tea in late winter and early spring. What is needed are herbs that stimulate and heal the metabolic processes of the queen as well as the workers. We have achieved good results with the following formula:

Prepare a mild tea by pouring boiling water over a mixture of
chamomile, yarrow and dandelion flowers, leaves (and stems) of
peppermint, rue, hyssop, horse tail, stinging nettle and thyme.
Tea made of oak bark that has been soaked overnight can then

Chamomile in bloom

be added to the other tea. Sweeten this with just enough spring flower honey to make it palatable for the bees. Two or three such tea offerings are enough to strengthen their intestinal and metabolic functions. These teas should not be overpowering. You should be able to drink them yourself. Homeopathic amounts are usually more effective in their stimulating function than 'sledge–hammer' solutions. (The same holds true for human consumption, of course.) Certainly other healing herbs native to the American continent can be added.

One more factor contributing to the foulbrood problem must be mentioned: the lack of hive warmth in early spring, especially March and April. It is better for the bees to be too warm at that time rather than too cool which can happen when supers are impatiently added to possibly prevent the 'danger' of swarming. This practice, at best, is able to postpone swarming. In addition, it can be very stressful for the colony when the weather suddenly turns cold in April and the brood has to be kept warm. This under–cooling of the brood can be seen as a critical factor in the colony's susceptibility for foulbrood. Isn't it true that in our country we cherish coolness: in our drinks, in our clothing, in our homes and cars? We should keep in mind that warmth is beneficial, even critical, for healthy development. Whereas our head can take quite a bit of coldness (keep a cool head!), our feet and abdomen – the areas of intense metabolism – need warmth to stay healthy. When they cool off too much, we are in danger of catching a cold, to which we react with a warming fever as a healing process. Likewise, one can consider the brood as an integral part of the metabolic processes, which definitely need warmth to stay healthy. Considering such basic facts, I can say that in over twenty years of keeping bees I have never given my colonies medication against foulbrood, and up till now have never had one case. (See Appendix B on how the foulbrood-infected colonies of beekeeper friends were successfully healed.)

How challenging beekeeping has become in our days! All that we have to learn and consider! So much attention must be given to illness and the kind of environment needed for healthy growth and thriving. And yet we do have a hopeful although limited repertoire of beneficial treatments!

WHAT IS THE CURE? Suppose we start all over again, and begin to internalize the cause of the bees' distress and try to rebuild the health of the honeybee from within? Perhaps the real cause of 'dis–ease' and the entry of mites, foulbrood and chalk brood can be truly prevented – or at least greatly reduced – by facilitating true 'ease' once again into every facet of the bees' life expressions.

Let's establish a new set of standards for working with the honeybee, that respect its very being and try to cater to its needs:

- **provide a comfortable home made of natural materials (no plastics and, if at all possible, no iron in the hive);**
- **allow natural procreation for queens;**
- **allow only the best sources of nourishment: honey and pollen;**
- **permit the autonomous creation of honeycomb to a great degree, thereby permitting as many drones as the colony wants and needs;**
- **provide an environment free of pesticides, antibiotics, plastic, substitutes for honey and pollen, and unnecessary intrusion;**
- **respect the colony as an organism rather than a mechanism with exchangeable parts.**

Some of these factors are, of course, not determined solely by the beekeeper and depend on the insight and good will of farmers, gardeners and lawn owners. In addition to the above-mentioned critical factors, each beekeeper should seriously pose the following questions:

Do we really have to ship our bees from one monoculture to another? Shouldn't every serious and responsible orchardist, farmer and gardener keep bees all year 'round, enjoying their benefits but also taking care of their needs? A deep satisfaction will be experienced in this activity.

Do we really need to work with blowers and chemicals designed to drive the bees away from their provisions in order to take honey from them? I've conducted workshops where each of fifty persons drew a frame or two, shook or gently brushed off the bees, set the honey frame into a box – all without veil or gloves! No one got stung. The attitude makes all the difference.

Do we really need to ship queens around the continent and beyond just as we ship spark plugs and light bulbs? Can we begin to respect the socialized intimacy that is an inherent part of the miraculous relationship between the queen and her workers?

Do we really need to tear apart the brood nest, and then proceed to hang in empty frames to speed up comb production? Can't we respect the brood nest as we respect the uterus of a mother–to–be? (Or have we forgotten that, too?)

There is much to consider if we truly want to support and restore our ailing bees to a level of vitality in which they can, once again, begin to flourish and thrive. This shift in attitude from a functional, profit–oriented, mechanical approach to a spiritual, organic one on the basis of heartfelt reverence is absolutely necessary if we want to keep that small but mighty animal who has served us and nature as a whole so diligently, over many millennia.

---

1) Oral information of an Oregon beekeeper to Ron Breland, beekeeper in Rockland County; official numbers are difficult to obtain since neither all colonies nor all losses are registered.
2) Webster's Encyclopedic Unabridged Dictionary of the English Language (1983) notes that 'dis-' is "a learned borrowing from Latin meaning 'apart', 'asunder',..."
3) Vereinigung fuer Wesensgemaesse Bienenhaltung, E.V.

7

Outlook

A barometer is a wonderful and sometimes even life-saving invention, indicating levels of pressure. I have come to think that the honeybee is such a delicate barometer. The pressure on all forms of life on this planet has reached a critical point at the dawn of the new millennium. Plant species are becoming extinct by the thousands each year; animal species are dying by the hundreds; the elements are polluted and poisoned; millions of tons of topsoil are lost each year. And only a small fraction of the population is concerned enough to make changes in demands and lifestyle that will, in turn, begin to heal our ailing environment.

If this continues – if there is no reversal in our ways of relating to nature – then unforeseen catastrophes will, without doubt, force us to wake up and to reconsider our ways. Day by day we are discovering more details about the extraordinarily complex interconnection of all life on this planet, an interconnection that reaches out, as well, to the vast distances of our cosmos. But we are slow enough in putting our knowledge to good use.

A tremendous shift in paradigm is needed at this time; one no less in importance or magnitude than the shift 500 years ago when the age of modernism and the dawning of technology began with Leonardo da Vinci. He stood at the crossroads: with one foot right in the center of deep spiritual perception and conception; he was part of a world mindset that placed God at the center as divine creator, a mindset which revered all divinities and supersensible beings as providers and caretakers of the physical realm. With the other foot he set out to discover the physical properties and laws in practically all realms of life, inventing gadgets and instruments so advanced that the technology needed to make them workable took four, even five centuries to develop.

Leonardo, then, was at the outset of man beginning to experience and assert the Ego–personality in a new way. It was now time to inquire, to question, to create and re–create physical reality rather than to merely 'take' what was given 'from Above'. This new orientation was to change civilization in a magnificent and irreversible way.

By now, we have made great strides in creating and controlling our own reality and we have gone a step farther. The virtual reality we have created is an unreal reality; and this new frontier challenges us in an unprecedented way. We have reached, and even passed, the threshold of the natural world perceived by our senses. Who can perceive all the waves, all the radiation that go through us every second, whether macro or micro? Who can perceive the consequences of our continued exploration into realms that surpass and in some ways defy the human senses?

The call is for us to broaden our minds and scope, to investigate supersensible realms by developing spiritual organs...spiritual ways of perceiving what lies beyond the complexity of physical life (Steiner 1994). We have discovered and investigated vast amounts of detail regarding the physical world. Just looking at the intricacy of what is presently known about photosynthesis or about the physiology and behavior of bees is overwhelming. This mountain of detailed knowledge has not helped us solve our environmental or social problems. On the contrary, these storehouses of information actually serve to hide from our glance the essential: *Life itself!* We can't see the woods for the trees anymore. Does the scientist researching ever more details have the ability to put the microscope aside and look at the object of his investigation with awe and wonder, with reverence and, above all, with love? A great educator, historian, writer, and doctor of the twentieth century, Walter Johannes Stein, once said:

> It is not the science about nature that allows us to lift the veil of secrets inherent in nature; rather it will be the gradual perfection of our own ability to love, which permits us by and by to lift it (Stein 1984).

Have we become so engrossed with accumulating so many details that we are actually unable to consolidate them into a living, meaningful Gestalt – an accessible, working image of the whole? It seems to me that only with a view of the whole, with a 'Weltanschauung' that can truly integrate the fragmented and specialized knowledge of the physical world with the uniting and healing depth of spiritual realities, will we be able to work out of a vision that lets us become responsible, (i.e. knowledgeable) co–creators. This will be the fulfillment of our innate right to strive for 'the pursuit of happiness'. Perhaps we should substitute 'deep inner joy' for 'happiness' to express what it means to live and work *with* nature as a caretaker and steward of life.

How can we accomplish this? With tools that are as simple as they are difficult: with newly acquired awe, respect, reverence, gratitude and wonder for all that exists in our life on earth and beyond. Simple? Perhaps, because it is a straightforward answer. Why difficult? Because we, in our fast–paced materialistically oriented times, are not normally raised with these virtues. How often do we stop to admire a blade of grass, a caterpillar, a brook, a tree, or a bee – let alone a mosquito?

Aren't we taught to wipe out, step on, squash, eradicate or kill whatever we don't understand as having purpose and meaning; or to see other beings only from our vantage point of comfort, ease, or fun? (Lauck 1998)

Our awakening, our reversal and new sense of direction will have to evolve through extensive communication and education. This is a difficult task because most of the teachers have to relearn for themselves, have to be inspired with new attitudes, deeper insights and fresh enthusiasm before they can inspire their students. The necessary change will partially be brought about simply by 'having our fill' of environmental and immunological suffering: the smog, the rising allergies and lung problems; the polluted drinking water; the sharp increase in nervous and neurological disorders, the influx of strange diseases and viruses, and so on.

Yet there is hope! Older and younger generations are indeed uniting with a new awareness and sense of responsibility for the earth and its inhabitants. Individuals are now courageous enough to risk their lives to save animals and plants; they are bold enough to stand up to large corporations, fighting for those beings that are not able to protect themselves. This new paradigm is what more and more individuals are now seeking. The material world, comprised solely of the physical discoveries

Midwinter dreams

and materialistic accomplishments does no longer give complete satisfaction. It is really the spirit that is sought in and through this world of matter. And it can be found. And when it is found, embraced and utilized to its full extent, it will transform our will so that we can fulfill our tasks as true caretakers and stewards for a creation that, as part of the universe, is experiencing evolution as well.

The renewal will not come through a major organizational shift at first; this can be said with safe assumption. In beekeeping it will probably not come through the beekeeping industry and the professionals. It will come about, just like organic agriculture, through individuals not blinded by accomplishments of technology and progress in the material sense; individuals who know or sense that there is more to life than what meets the eye; individuals who have an innate interest and love for all living beings: plants, animals and human companions (the word 'compan-ion' means the one with whom you share your bread!).

Such individuals will support and practice a truly holistic way of looking at the world, a way that encompasses the microcosm and the macrocosm, a way that unites, rather than separates the material *and* the spiritual. The ever more specialized and isolated thinking developed over the last 500 years will be gradually overcome.

In respect to our honeybee, the present-day hope of breeding a bee that is resistant to the varroa mite, is an example of the old way of thinking, of selecting only one factor out of a totality of factors influencing and determining an organic whole. One scientist, the professor at the Entomology department at the University of Hohenheim in Germany, exposes the shortsightedness of such thinking: "Besides, in trying to select a resistance or tolerance to the varroa mite, it must be kept in mind that such a selection in the honeybee results in a corresponding selection of the varroa mite. In this race the varroa has, without a doubt, the advantage. The varroa problem cannot be solved by breeding, by selection.... It would be more probable that the problem solve itself on its own. And that is improbable." (Liebig 1996, 363–368)

This is a clear statement: *the problem won't solve itself on its own.* And we can say that we can't solve a problem staying within the same mindset that created it. Certainly it won't be solved by singling out one factor, hoping to find the 'silver bullet'. We need to raise our awareness and out of a new, more holistic way of perceiving, take initiative in turning the tide. We have to become individuals of good will; and this good will reveals itself in deeds. Deeds that come out of the warmth of an awakened conscience, out of a morality that includes the responsibility of stewardship for all that exists on earth. That means that we won't evaluate the other being's worth according to our gain and treat them disrespectfully.

Advertisements like the following will be felt to be immoral:

"WE ASKED SOME BEES WHAT WOULD MAKE THEM MORE PROFITABLE." (Mann Lake Ltd. 2001)

The true essence of the bee (the Spiritual Bee) is waiting for individuals to ask the bees: "What would make you more comfortable; what do you need for your well-being and health?" It is waiting for beekeepers *not intent on robbing* the bee but respecting its own needs, taking graciously of the surplus honey, a gift it readily shares with us. Not only the bees, but rather all our domestic (and wild) animals are waiting for more and more farmers and land stewards to give them a home on our Earth in which they can thrive and be respected. All this requires the good will to serve rather than the desire to control. Control –

whether political, economical, or spiritual – renders only short-term solutions before reactions set in, often powerful and destructive. The twentieth century gave ample documentation for this truth and as yet, the twenty-first century shows little has changed. When will we ever learn?!

At this time, I cannot ward off the feeling that the bee itself is in despair for the general misuse and mistreatment of her colonies. It is withdrawing, unable to give of her blessings because she is simply exhausted by our exploitation.

Let us consider, in our mind and heart, a renewed approach of reverence and care for all of our earth's creatures. Let us help the honeybee regain her health and joy of living.

Busy at the round hive

Appendix A
Formic, Oxalic, &
Lactic Acid Treatments

Formic acid has been in use as a miticide for over two decades and much testing has gone into its application. It is usually bought in an 85 perecnt dilution and has to be further diluted with clear water down to 60–65 percent since damage to the bees and queen losses have been experienced with full strength application. The diluting is easily done by adding half the amount of water, i.e., mixing 5 ounces of water into 10 ounces of 85 percent formic acid will give you the right strength. In the United States, the commercially available package form (introduced in 2000) was taken off the market within a few months because the packages leaked. It can be hoped that it will be sold again soon in an improved form. Up to the date of publishing this book, no other way of using it has been approved in the USA, and the following explanation simply attempts to record my own experiences and those of other European researchers, and is not to be taken as advice to go against present laws. On the other hand, the research in Europe was and still is carried out by private individuals or organizations who do not want to wait until they get the finished and approved results from our chemical companies.

The effectiveness of formic acid lies by about 100 percent in killing off tracheal mites. On varroa mites it varies between 60 percent and 95 percent according to outside temperature, to the hive strength, to the rate of evaporation, as well as to factors as yet undetermined. Its real advantage lies in its being able to penetrate the wax capping of the brood and becoming effective not only in the bee population outside of the capped cells. Therefore it can be used in all seasons.

The procedure is simple but has to be executed with utmost care, since the acid is quite caustic, burns the skin and can cause serious injury. In twenty years of applying it I have not been hurt, however, and have not heard of anyone suffering injury. The formic acid is put on a soft press-board or a double layer of cardboard (a fellow beekeeper in Wisconsin said he had good results using a feminine pad!) which is put into a plastic bag over night so that there is even distribution. The board is inserted in the hive on top of the frames after smoking the bees so they don't come into direct contact with the acid. This pad or sheet is then left in the hive for three to seven days. The absorbent material should be thick enough to prevent the acid from evaporating too quickly to prevent causing damage to the bees. The ideal temperature for using it ranges from 50–75 degrees F. At lower temperatures the rate of evaporation slows down, at higher temperatures the acid may evaporate too fast. On warmer days, when the temperature rises above 75 degrees F., I always insert it in late evening to prevent a too rapid evaporation; at times or in climates where it does not cool off significantly over night, it is advisable to put the acid–soaked material below the frames. Ideally half an ounce of liquid should evaporate per day. This can be checked more easily with the commercially available applicators like the Nassenheimer applicator.

The dosage that many researchers have found to work well is one ounce of 65 percent acid per nine or ten frames (one deep hive body), but never more than two ounces, even if the number of frames in a hive exceeds eighteen.

Formic acid neither accumulates in the wax nor in the honey. In a very low, homeopathic dilution it is part of the bee's own body, especially the poison and permeates the entire hive. Nevertheless, it is advisable not to do an application within a month of honey–extraction, just to be on the safe side. Four treatments with one–week intervals between August and October have proven to be very effective. With careful handling there are no queen losses.

It should be self–evident that protective gear has to be worn when working with the acid (rubber gloves and a face mask) and that it has to be kept out of reach of children.

Fortunately the ideas of integrated pest management are also spreading, slowly but surely, into beekeeping circles. That means that any treatments against mites are not just made routinely, but according to need. Ideal is the monitoring of mite population with a commercially available varroa screen and tray so that no superfluous treatments are made. For almost two decades we made our own screens or used simple cardboards with edges smeared with shortening and the whole thing was covered with fly screen. It's a bit easier now, although a little more expensive. When should we make a treatment? When the natural death rate of two to three mites per day is reached; then you know that you have anywhere between 300 and 600 mites in the hive. Since the mite population doubles or triples approximately every two weeks, depending on season, weather and individual colony, you will soon have many damaged bees emerging from their cells and the secondary infections will add to the dilemma and can cause a rather sudden collapse of the colony in late summer, early fall. You can imagine that two or three mites dying naturally in March present a more serious threat than the same number in October, with the brood nest declining.

In addition to the formic acid, *oxalic acid* has been researched in Europe as a treatment against mites. In the late 1980s I heard of the pioneer work carried out by Thomas Radetzki and his staff at the Mellifera e.V., Vereinigung fuer wesensgemaesse Bienen-haltung (Association for Keeping Bees in Accordance to Their Nature) at the Fischermuehle in Rosenfeld, Germany (e-mail: <info@mellifera.de>; website: <www.mellifera.de>). They have perfected the mode of application and tested the effectiveness and safety for the bees in over a decade of diligent work. For many years now they have been working together with the entomo-logical research department headed by Dr. Gerhard Liebig at the University Hohenheim, Stuttgart, Germany (Landesanstalt fuer Bienenkunde der Universitaet Hohenheim). Their latest development is an aerosol applicator that enables the beekeeper to make a treatment with oxalic acid without opening the hive. Hopefully this method will be approved by the FDA and made available very soon in North America.

Oxalic acid also is a naturally occurring acid, of utmost importance in all life processes. Not only is it part of our own metabolic processes, but in extremely fine dilution it is present in all plants. In some it is more perceptible, like in oxalic clover, rhubarb and sorrel.

For treatment against varroa mites it is used in a 2.1 percent chemical dilution. For example, one ounce of acid crystals is diluted with one quart of tap water. As with the formic acid, it is absolutely necessary to use the same protective measures, including face mask (in this case also protecting the eyes, since the acid is sprayed) and rubber gloves.

One great advantage in using the oxalic acid is its low concentration, another its extreme effectiveness. With proper application, the sprays can be as great as 98 percent effective! The great disadvantage, however, lies in the fact that is does not penetrate the brood cappings; that means it will only kill the mites outside the capped brood. Therefore the applications with the excellent results are limited to times when there is no capped brood in the hive:

• after swarming, when the swarm has built comb and has only uncapped brood; and when the young queen has begun to lay eggs but the brood from the old queen has emerged from the cells.

• In the winter, when there is a brood interruption. The outside temperature should be at least 50–55 degrees F. In other words the bees should be flying. In December one can usually still capture a few days that allow one to open the hive and carry out the procedure. In warmer climates this presents a problem, since the bees can have brood all year long.

The procedure is not as easy as with the formic acid, for the frames have to be drawn and each frame with bees given a mild spray. For the sensitive beekeeper this presents a problem: open the hive in December, draw each frame with bees and put the frame back? "Not for me", most beekeepers would say. It really takes a bit of overcoming one's instinct and feeling to go ahead and disturb the bees at this time. And yet, in fifteen years of doing this, I have not lost one hive to the oxalic acid treatment and the bees are gentle and don't react with aggressiveness. Maybe one has to let them know that the disturbance is to their benefit. Other forms of applying the acid, like gently pouring it into the hive of with some kind of applicator, have not proven effective enough or have caused queen losses. The new aerosol applicator (sold by the Swiss firm Andermatt BIOCONTROL AG; e-mail: <sales@biocontrol.ch>; website: <www.biocontrol.ch>) is really a great improvement, combining the acid's effectiveness with the benefit of not having to open the hive at this time of year.

Whether in summer or winter, give the bees a good smoking before you start the application. If you use the spray method, draw each frame with bees and also spray inside walls of the hive. The spray should be very fine; bees must not get wet (you need a good quality sprayer.)

Spray one ounce of the liquid oxalic acid on both sides of approximately ten frames of bees.

Be aware of wind direction and spray with the wind for your protection. It's a good idea to first try out with water to determine how many squeezes give an ounce of water into a measuring glass; then divide by ten to know how many squeezes are needed per frame of bees. My experience is that two light squeezes on the sprayer's trigger side give you approximately the right amount for a frame. In formal tests, no residues have been found either in honey or wax.

In closing, it must be stated again that the greatest precaution against inhaling the fumes must be taken, and since this is not a treatment legalized by the FDA, experiments are made at the beekeeper's own risk and responsibility.

A third acid that has been used in the attempt to control the damage caused by the varroa mite is *lactic acid*. Personally I do not have any experience with it but have read about the good results some European beekeepers have had with it.

What is needed is a 15–18 percent dilution. The bees are finely sprayed (no wet bees!) four to five times a year. As with the oxalic acid, each frame has to be drawn for that procedure. This treatment is possible at all times. As with the other two acids, it leaves no residues in wax or honey. Three treatments in spring have shown to give a good protection against varroa mites. A winter treatment (in November or December on a warmer day, above 50 degrees F) without brood is supposed to be up to 99 percent effective in getting rid of the mites.

Lactic acid and its health–imbuing properties are well known in human nutrition. Many illnesses are said to have been cured with lactic acid fermented vegetables. Sauerkraut is probably the best known, but other vegetables can also be fermented and are part of the daily diet in some cultures. Lactic acid evokes images of the rich nourishing and fertility creating benefits we derive from the cow. Maybe this is a substance that shows greater promise than merely aiding the bee in her plight with the mites.

Using lactic acid seems to be also a relatively mild form of dealing with the mites, but it definitely needs more research. Be careful, though! It, too, is an acid!

All three acids in their use against the mites are by no means the final answer, the silver bullet. They are, in my opinion, a means to help the bees survive until they gather renewed strength and vitality to take on the battle by themselves. More spiritual research and applied practices deriving from it are needed in the long run if we are to keep our bees; if we are to be fortunate enough to be keepers of bees.

Appendix B
Foulbrood

The bacillus larvae cause this disease. As was discussed in chapter six, an infectious disease is not automatically caused by any specific bacteria, fungus or virus, but the decisive factor is rather the combination of ideal conditions it finds for growth and reproduction. The same holds true for the illnesses that befall the bees. When the imminent strength of immunity is present in an organism, then all the known 'culprits' can be around but will have no effect.

So let us summarize the most important factors responsible for foulbrood. Since this disease affects the brood rather than the adult bee, we should first consider the metabolic functions, primarily the food for both the brood and the queen, to find weakening factors. First of all, let's take a look at the queen. She is fed a good amount of high-protein food, the royal jelly, which enables her to lay such an enormous amount of eggs a day. It is this food, transformed in her body, which invigorates her metabolism to produce a constant stream of eggs, up to 1500 each day at the height of the season.

On the one hand, we can pose the question what quality of nourishment is available in nature. In view of the mindless poisoning of not only our agricultural products, but also our flora and fauna with all the pesticides, insecticides, fungicides and herbicides, the available bee forage is definitely of a poor, sometimes even illness-producing quality. The monoculture crops which our commercial colonies are asked to pollinate only add to the problem. The great variety of herbs and weeds that used to enrich and enliven our landscapes has been radically diminished or is totally missing. Where do we still see bachelor buttons or poppies decorating our fields? Even our pastures have turned into monocultures of grasses, lacking the healing benefits of wild oregano, thyme, dandelion and their companions. These 'weeds' have always been a source of health for our bees. To top it off, pollen substitutes (usually soybean products) are often given in spring to push the queen into a quicker egg production. Nothing, but really nothing, can take the place of pollen itself, as we have discussed! With the hedges that adorned the borders of the fields gone, the filbert, hawthorn and pussy willow have become rare. They were major sources of pollen in early spring, a natural boost that enabled bees to quickly build up their colonies.

On the other hand, a second major factor in the degraded food source is the sugar feeding that is recommended in every modern beekeeping manual and bee journal. Alas, I have not encountered many beekeepers who question this practice. We are so used to taking all the honey we can get and don't think twice about giving sugar as a substitute. We have discussed in detail the stress and imbalance this creates for our bees.

Both the environmental factors and the sugar feeding have disturbed delicate balances in the bees' metabolic system and have undermined her immune system. We can safely assume that the food given to the queen as well as to the brood is of inferior quality, and we can surmise that this brood can have an inherent weakness and susceptibility to fungus or bacterial attacks.

Yet a third factor can be found that has a powerful impact on the honeybee's health and immune system. We have to look at the queen breeding process itself. As described, inferiority has been bred into our colonies. Do the attempts to raise 'pure-bred' bees also play into this picture? Not only with plants, but also dogs, cats and horses we know that the more pure-bred they become – the more refined, one could say – the more susceptible to disease and illness they become.

Rudolf Steiner, in answer to a question R. Hahn posed in regard to foulbrood, suggested, "probably the faulty creation of uric acid is the cause of the disease" (Steiner 1998, 178).

Uric acid is, of course, intimately interrelated with the processes of metabolism, especially with nitrogen. One can safely assume that the standard overfertilization of our fields with

74

nitrogen has its subtle and yet powerful influence on this process. This is something that will have to be investigated. One thing is sure: all the environmental problems and detrimental beekeeping practices mentioned before are part of the cause for the susceptibility to foulbrood and other diseases.

What can we do to help? Avoid as many of these practices, is one suggestion. In addition, we can strengthen and heal the metabolic processes with herb teas as described in Chapter Six.

The warmth factor in the early spring, especially March and April, should also be considered. All these considerations, which take the honeybees' own needs into our awareness and beekeeping practice, will in due time help our bees gather strength to better ward off the diseases.

Since I have never had a case of foulbrood in my colonies, I can only tell you how I have helped save a friend's colony infected with this disease following a method described in Matthias Thun's book *Die Biene, Haltung und Pflege*. One must remember that the bacterium is practically in every colony in your apiary if you have an infected colony. But only the weak ones will succumb to the infection.

So here is what you can do, if it does not go against your state's laws:

In the early evening, when most of the bees are in the hive, you give your colony repeated puffs of smoke, waiting a few minutes until the bees have taken up a good amount of honey as provision. Then carefully shake all the bees off the frames – a little spraying with water helps – into a clean hive body that has an entrance guard in place that prevents any bee from leaving. The empty frames are put back into the original hive and any bees that will still gather in it will have to be fumigated later on in the evening. The new hive body should have a few empty frames so that the bees can start building comb in the next few days. The bees are put into a cool, quiet, dark place (perhaps a cellar) for forty-eight hours, where they will use up their provisions and begin to get hungry. Then they will clean each other from remnants of honey and in this process imbibe the foulbrood spores. These cannot survive in the bees' stomach and thus their numbers are greatly reduced. Personally I don't assume that there is a complete cleansing of spores possible, but the pressure is greatly reduced to a point where the bees can handle it.

After this quarantine, the frames with the bees are lifted into a clean hive body (care is taken not to get any of the droppings lying on the floor into the new hive) and extra frames are added with perhaps one-inch strips of foundation to guide the comb building. If there isn't a good honey flow at the time, the colony will have to be fed with honey, not sugar. The renewed activity of building their own comb with predominantly their very own wax is, in itself, a source of strength and healing.

The colony thus treated not only regained its strength and survived the year, but also the following hard winter. If the foulbrood is discovered in fall in a temperate climate, the colonies will have to be destroyed since they cannot build up anew at this time. Needless to say, the normal precautions suggested with foulbrood-infested hives need to be heeded; i.e., wax and frames must either burned or buried three or more feet deep, and the hive body must either be flamed thoroughly, burned or buried.

References

ADIZ, i.e., Allgemeine Deutsche Imker Zeitung. 2000; 11:9–11

Anderson, Curt. 07/07/98. *AP Online*.

Berry, Wendell. 1981. *The Gift of Good Land*. New York: North Point Press.

Carson, Rachel. 1962. *Silent Spring*. Boston: Houghton Mifflin.

von Goethe, Johann Wolfgang. 1902. *Truth and Fiction*. Boston: Francis A. Niccols and Company.

Herold, Edmund. 1970. *Heilwerte aus dem Bienenvolk*. Munich: Ehrenwirth Verlag.

Holdrege, Craig. 1996. *Genetics and the Manipulation of Life*. Hudson, NY: Lindisfarne Press.

Liebig, Dr. Gerhard. 1996. *Bienenpflege*. 12:363–368

———. 1999. *Alternative Varroabekaempfung*. Stuttgart: Landesanstalt fuer Bienenkunde der Universitaet Hohenheim. (Also published by Eidgenoessische Forschunganstalt fuer Milchwirtschaft/Sektion Bienen.)

Lauck, Joann E. 1998. *The Voice of the Infinite in the Small*. Mill Spring, NC: Swan, Raven and Company.

Kolisko, Eugen and Lili. 1978. *Agriculture of Tomorrow*. Bournemouth, England: The Acorn Press.

Mann Lake Ltd. 2001. *Catalog of Beekeeping and Candlemaking Supplies*.

Maeterlinck, Maurice. 1915. *The Life of the Bee*. New York: Dodd, Mead and Company.

Mancke, Guenther and Peter Csarnietzki. 1996. *Der Weissenseifener Haengekorb*. Weissenseifen–Michaelshag: Werkgemeinschaft Kunst und Heilpaedagogik.

Pfeiffer, Ehrenfried. 1983. *Biodynamic Gardening and Farming*, Volume 1. Spring Valley, NY: Mercury Press.

Stein, Walter Johannes. 1984. *The Death of Merlin*. Edinburgh: Floris Books.

Steiner, Rudolf. 1993. *Agriculture*. Kimberton, PA: Biodynamic Farming and Gardening Association.

———. 1998. *Bees*. Hudson, New York: Anthroposophic Press.

———. 2000. *From Comets to Cocaine*. London: Rudolf Steiner Press.

———. 1994. *How to Know Higher Worlds*. New York: Anthroposophic Press.

Thun, Matthias. 1986. *Die Biene, Haltung und Pflege*. Biedenkopf, Germany: Aussaattage M. Thun-Verlag.

Weiler, Michael. 1996. *Der Mensch und die Bienen*. Darmstadt: Verlag Lebendige Erde.

About the Author

Günther Hauk, an educator of long-standing and a biodynamic gardener and beekeeper for over twenty-five years, works with beekeepers in the United States and abroad, investigating ways of keeping bees that would strengthen and improve their natural health and resistance to diseases and parasites. Turning the tide of the honeybee's spiraling death rate is a task dear to his heart.

He is Director of the Biodynamic Gardening and Environmental Studies program of the Pfeiffer Center in Chestnut Ridge, New York.

Production Notes

The text face and headings are Nofret, designed by Gudrun Zapf–von Hesse and issued by Berthold. To quote Robert Bringhurst from *The Elements of Typographic Style*, Nofret, "which is named for Nefertiti, is a queenly face". As such, it seems an appropriate choice for this book.

Layout, composition and production by Bruce Bumbarger

Cover design by Dale Hushbeck

Printed by Thomson–Shore, Dexter MI